THE
NAPOLEONIC
WARS

THE NAPOLEONIC WARS

GUNTHER E. ROTHENBERG

Series Editor, John Keegan

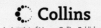

Smithsonian Books

Collins

An Imprint of HarperCollinsPublishers

Text © 1999 by Gunther E. Rothenberg
Design and layout © Cassell
The picture credits on p. 240 constitute an extension to this copyright page.
First published in Great Britain, 1999
Reprinted 2000
UK paperback edition 2002
This paperback edition 2006

Published 2006 in the United States of America by Smithsonian Books
In association with Cassell
Wellington House, 125 Strand
London, WC2R 0BB

Library of Congress Cataloging-in-Publication Data has been applied for.
ISBN-10: 0-06-085121-X
ISBN-13: 978-0-06-085121-7

Manufactured in Spain, not at government expense.

Title page: *Napoleon issues final orders to his corps commanders before the
fighting begins at Austerlitz.*

Overleaf: *A typical grognard of the Old Guard Grenadiers, with his unit,
exchanging fire prior to the assault. Bayonets were commonly carried fixed,
but inflicted few casualties, as one or the other side would give way.*

Acknowledgements

I gratefully acknowledge the help and comfort provided by my wife, Dr Eleanor I. M. Hancock, during the writing of this book. Also, I wish to thank Caroline Knight and Penny Gardiner, both at Orion, whose cheerful good humour and enthusiasm encouraged me when my spirits were flagging. May all authors have the good fortune to enjoy such support.

Gunther Rothenberg
Monash University

J. Bastin

Contents

KEY TO MAPS

Military units–types

infantry

cavalry

Military units–size

NAPOLEON   army commander

XXXX
army

XXX
corps

XX
division

X
brigade

cavalry

infantry

III
regiment

II
battalion

Military movements

→ attack

-→ retreat

Commanders

French

British

Prussian

Russian

Austrian

General military symbols

✕ site of battle

▟ fort

● ● ●   skirmish line

⇌ field gun

Military unit colours
unless otherwise shown

French

Allies

Geographical symbols

settlement

settlement (3D maps)

——— road

——— river

– – – seasonal river

⋯⋯ canal

——— border

≍ bridge

≈ ford

Map list

Chronology of the Napoleonic Wars

1792

20 April	French Assembly declares war on Austria.
15 May	France declares war on Piedmont.
26 June	First Coalition formed.
20 Sept	Battle of Valmy.
6 Nov	Austrians defeated at Jemappes.

1793

1 Feb	Convention declares war on Britain and Holland.
20 Feb	Convention calls up 300,000 conscripts.
9 March	Convention declares war on Spain.
23 August	Committee of Public Safety decrees *levée en masse*.
16 Sept	Bonaparte takes charge of artillery before Toulon.
19 Dec	Toulon falls.
22 Dec	Bonaparte promoted to brigadier general.

1794

26 June	Defeat at Fleurus forces Austrians to evacuate Belgium.
27 July	Overthrow of radical Committee of Public Safety.

1795

16 May	Peace of Basle, Prussia leaves war.
19 August	Peace with Spain.
5 Oct	Bonaparte puts down attempted coup.

1796

1 March	Directoire appoints Bonaparte commander Army of Italy.
27 March	Bonaparte assumes command.
10–22 April	Bonaparte's offensive against Austro-Piedmont.
28 April	Piedmont sign armistice.
10 May	Action at Lodi.
15 May	Milan occupied.
4 June	Investment of Mantua (lifted 31 July).
2–5 August	Battles of Lonato and Castiglione.
1–12 Sept	Würmser breaks through to Mantua.
3 Sept	French defeated at Würzburg.
8 Oct	Spain declares war on Britain.
15–17 Nov	Battle of Arcola.

1797

14 Jan	Battle of Rivoli.
2 Feb	Mantua surrenders.
18 April	Armistice of Leoben.
17 Oct	Treaty of Campo Formio with Austria.

1798

12 April	Bonaparte appointed commander Army of the Orient.
1 July	Bonaparte lands at Alexandria.
21 July	Battle of the Pyramids.
1 August	Nelson destroys French fleet at Aboukir.
21 Oct	Cairo revolt suppressed.
29 Dec	Second Coalition formed.

1799

29 Jan	French occupy Naples.
6 Feb	Bonaparte invades Palestine.
1 March	Russia declares war on France.
17 Mar–20 May	Siege of Acre.
25 March	Archduke Charles defeats French at Stockach.
5 April–15 Aug	Austro-Russian forces recapture Italy and Switzerland.
25 July	Bonaparte smashes Turks at Aboukir.
23 August	Bonaparte sails for France.
27 Aug–19 Nov	Anglo-Russian landing in north Holland fails.
25–30 Sept	Massena defeats Russians near Zurich.
9–10 Nov	Coup establishes Consulate.
14 Dec	Bonaparte becomes First Consul.

1800

6 April	Austrian offensive in north-west Italy.
3 May	Moreau victorious at Stockach.
15–21 May	Army of Reserve crosses Alps.
14 June	Battle of Marengo.
3 Dec	Battle of Hohenlinden.
16 Dec	Northern (Armed Neutrality) League formed.

1801

9 Feb	Peace of Lunéville.
23 March	Tsar Paul murdered; Alexander succeeds.
2 April	British attack Copenhagen.
2 Sept	Army of the Orient capitulates.

1802

26 Jan	Italian Republic established; Bonaparte president.
25 March	Peace of Amiens.
11 Sept	France annexes Piedmont.
15 Oct	France invades Switzerland.

1803

16 May	Britain declares war on France.
1 June	French seize Hanover.
15 June	French army concentrates along Channel.

1804

21 March	Duc d'Enghien murdered.
18 May	Napoleon proclaimed Emperor.
19 May	Marshalate created.
2 Dec	Napoleon crowns himself.
14 Dec	Spain declares war on Britain.

1805

11 April	Anglo-Russian Alliance.
26 May	Napoleon crowns himself King of Italy.
7 June	Eugène appointed viceroy.
9 August	Austria joins Third Coalition.
27 August	Grande Armée marches for Danube.
9 Sept	Austria invades Bavaria.
7 Oct	French elements cross Danube.
20 Oct	Mack surrenders at Ulm.
14 Nov	Napoleon enters Vienna.
2 Dec	Napoleon victorious at Austerlitz.
26 Dec	Treaty of Pressburg.

1806

1 April	Joseph Bonaparte becomes King of Naples.
20 June	Louis Bonaparte declared King of Holland.
12 July	Confederation of the Rhine established.
9 August	Prussia mobilizes.
1 Oct	Prussian ultimatum to France.
6 Oct	Fourth Coalition formed.
7 Oct	French enter Saxony.
14 Oct	Battle of Jena–Auerstädt destroys Prussian Army.
26 Oct	Napoleon enters Berlin.

1807

8 Feb	Battle of Eylau.
18 Mar–27 May	Siege of Danzig.
13–14 June	Battle of Friedland.
7–9 July	Treaty of Tilsit.
2–7 Sept	British bombard Copenhagen, seize Danish fleet.
1 Dec	Junot occupies Lisbon.

1808

2 May	Murat represses Madrid rising.
6 June	Joseph Bonaparte proclaimed King of Spain.
9 June	Austria establishes Landwehr.
20 July	French corps capitulates at Baylen.
1 August	Wellesley lands Portugal.
21 August	Battle of Vimiero.
14 Oct	Erfurt Congress concludes.
27 Oct	Moore moves to operate in Spain.
5 Nov	Napoleon assumes command in Spain.
4 Dec	Napoleon smashes Spanish forces and enters Madrid.

1809

8 Jan	Austria decides on war.
16 Jan	Napoleon forces Moore to evacuate at Corunna.
9 April	Fifth Coalition formed.
10 April	Charles invades Bavaria.
20–24 April	Napoleon defeats Austrians in Bavaria in series of battles.
26 April	Wellesley returns to Portugal.
12 May	Battle of Oporto.
13 May	Napoleon enters Vienna.
21–22 May	Charles repulses Napoleon at Aspern–Essling.
14 June	Battle of Raab.
5–6 July	Battle of Wagram.
28 July	Battle of Talavera.
29 July–9 Dec	Abortive British expedition to Walcheren.
14 Oct	Peace at Schönbrunn.
20 Oct	Start construction Lines of Torres Vedras.

1810

17 April	Massena appointed commander Army of Portugal.
9 July	Massena takes Ciudad Rodrigo.
9 July	Napoleon annexes Holland.

28 August	Fall of Almeida.
27 Sept	Battle of Bussaco.
10 Oct	Massena's advance stalled by Lines of Torres Vedras.

1811

5 March	Massena begins withdrawal.
3–5 May	Battle of Fuentes de Oñoro.
16 May	Battle of Albuera.
23 Dec	Napoleon begins preparations to invade Russia.

1812

19 Jan	Wellington storms Ciudad Rodrigo.
6 April	Badajoz falls with shocking atrocities.
20 June	Sixth Coalition formed.
24 June	French cross Niemen into Russia.
22 July	Battle of Salamanca.
12 August	Wellington enters Madrid.
17–19 August	Battle of Smolensk.
7 Sept	Napoleon defeats Kutuzov at Borodino.
9 Sept–18 Oct	Wellington's siege of Burgos fails.
14 Sept	Napoleon enters Moscow.
19 Oct	Napoleon evacuates Moscow.
24–25 Oct	Battle at Maloyaroslavets.
19 Nov	Wellington falls back to Portuguese frontier.
26–28 Nov	Battle of the Beresina.
5 Dec	Napoleon abandons army.
14 Dec	Last French elements leave Russia.
30 Dec	Yorck signs Convention of Tauroggen neutralizing his corps.

1813

4 March	Russians enter Berlin.
16 March	Prussia declares war on France.
2 May	Napoleon defeats Russo-Prussian army at Grossgörschen.
18 May	Bernadotte and Swedish troops land.
20–21 May	Napoleon defeats Russo-Prussians at Bautzen.
23 May	Wellington advances into Spain.
4 June–17 Aug	Armistice of Pleischwitz.
12 June	French evacuate Madrid.
21 June	Wellington's victory at Vitoria.
27 June	Austria joins Russia and Prussia.

12 August	Austria declares war on France.
23 August	Battle at Grossbeeren.
26 August	Macdonald defeated on the Katzbach.
26–27 August	Napoleon defeats Schwarzenberg at Dresden.
6 Sept	Ney defeated at Dennewitz.
8 Oct	Bavaria joins Allies in Treaty of Ried.
16–19 Oct	Combined allied armies defeat Napoleon at Leipzig.
18 Oct	Saxons defect to Allies during battle.
30 Oct	Napoleon defeats Bavarians at Hanau.
10 Nov	Battle of the Nivelle.

1814

11 Jan	Murat signs separate peace with Allies.
1 Feb	Blücher repels Napoleon.
10–14 Feb	Napoleon mauls Prussians at Champaubert, Montmirail and Vauchamps.
17–18 Feb	Napoleon defeats Schwarzenberg at Monterau.
9 March	Blücher defeats Marmont at Laon.
13 March	Napoleon victorious at Rheims.
20–21 March	Battle at Arcis-sur-Aube.
25 March	Engagement at Fère-Champenoise.
31 March	Allies enter Paris.
4 April	Marshals demand Napoleon's abdication.
6 April	Napoleon abdicates.
10 April	Wellington defeats Soult at Toulouse.

1815

26 Feb	Napoleon escapes from Elba.
20 March	Napoleon enters Paris.
25 March	Seventh Coalition formed.
31 March	Murat declares war on Austria.
3 May	Austrians defeat Murat at Tolentino.
15 June	Napoleon with Armée du Nord crosses into Belgium.
16 June	Napoleon defeats Blücher at Ligny.
16–17 June	Wellington delays Ney at Quatre Bras.
18 June	Grouchy engages Prussians at Wavre.
18 June	Wellington and Blücher defeat Napoleon at Waterloo.
22 June	Napoleon abdicates.

The Napoleonic Wars in the History of Warfare

Napoleon in his study wearing his favourite costume, the simple undress uniform – green coat with scarlet cuffs, collar and braiding, tight white pants and black boots – of a colonel of the Chasseurs à Cheval de la Garde Impériale.

The Napoleonic Wars in the History of Warfare

THIS BOOK FORMS PART of a multi-volume series on the history of warfare from the fourth millennium BC to the present. Specifically it deals with the Napoleonic Wars, the twelve years from 1803 to 1815. In this volume the focus is on the conduct of war; how armies were handled to achieve the overall objectives of policy. Much of this belongs to the strategic level, but operations and tactics in various theatres of war and in specific battles are included. In addition, the military establishments of the major participants in these wars are discussed.

Considerable space is given to Napoleon Bonaparte, General, Consul, and finally Emperor; one of the truly great commanders of history. The French Revolution gave him his opportunity and from it he inherited large armies led by young, unorthodox and aggressive commanders who under his leadership waged famous campaigns, establishing, if briefly, an empire from the Tagus to the Vistula. Though ultimately defeated, Napoleon not only stamped his way of waging war and his personal leadership on his own armies, but he compelled his adversaries to adopt military reforms to counter his genius. To understand this achievement the era of the Revolutionary and Napoleonic Wars must be placed within the context of what has become known as the 'military revolution'. This revolution, a major change in the way European states raised, trained, equipped and employed armies, has been variously dated, but can be said to have started in the period when more effective firearms, albeit still in combination with pikes, began to dominate the battlefield – that is, shortly after 1550. This revolution, it has been argued, extended into the eighteenth century and even included the Napoleonic Wars which are seen as the end, not as the beginning, of a new era.

This contention, however, is not accepted here. While as in all major conflicts there was a mixture of old and new, in several important aspects the wars of the French Revolution and even more the Napoleonic Wars constituted a clear break with the past and marked the origins of modern warfare. Never before had there been as total a mobilization of civilian as well as military resources leading to fundamental changes in the size and character of armies. Moreover, in contrast to the largely indecisive campaigns of the previous century, Napoleon's mass armies operated on a much larger scale with unprecedented speed and decisiveness. Though the Revolution had already unveiled a new way of war, the superiority of the French armies had not been absolute and they lost as many battles as they won. Only after Napoleon took power were there campaigns that within a short time led to great and decisive battles that became the idealized model for successive generations of commanding officers. In the end, of course, Napoleon was defeated. His desire for hegemony and concentration of personal power led to a strategic overreach and ultimately to his downfall. The overreach first became apparent in his attempts to bring Britain down by a system of economic warfare which in turn led to his invasion of the Iberian Peninsula, where after 1809 his commanders could not deal effectively with either Wellington's army or the British-supported guerrilla war.

By 1809, too, European powers were catching up with the Napoleonic way of war. All increased the size of their armies, adopted the corps as the main manoeuvre unit, improved their staffs and increased their artillery. And when in 1813 all major European powers combined, Napoleon was overthrown. His reputation as a great captain remained, however, and the combat methods evolved by the end of the Napoleonic Wars continued to be used well beyond the second quarter of the nineteenth century, even though the general introduction of rifled weapons created a dichotomy between firepower and tactics. The manoeuvres and tactics of the various European conflicts and of the American Civil War would have been perfectly familiar to any general of the Napoleonic era. Above all, Napoleon's influence was most apparent and longest lasting in military theory and on the operational and strategic level. Although Napoleon never wrote down his strategic concepts, once explaining that in war the 'simplest manoeuvres are the best', a considerable literature emerged trying to deduce meaningful patterns from his generalship. The most influential interpreter was Antoine Jomini, who had served on Ney's staff before deserting to the Russians, and whose many writings were prescribed reading in military academies. His influence was profound in the French army, while during the American Civil War generals on both sides 'advanced sword in one hand and a copy of Jomini in the other'.

The second major interpreter, Prussian military philosopher von Clausewitz, was far more sophisticated and complex, refusing to accept the validity of any fixed system and concentrating on the interaction of war, politics and society, concepts highly praised if rarely understood or practised. The mobilization of national armies sustained by popular will had, he held, become decisive in war. Both men emphasized the concentration of superior numbers and offensive action.

Meanwhile, the Industrial Revolution and the rapid development of railways and electric telegraphs allowed the deployment of huge armies capable of operating in Napoleonic patterns – unsuccessfully in the American Civil War, but successfully by the Prussian Helmuth von Moltke in 1866 and 1870–71. After this all continental general staffs adopted offensive war plans, expecting quick and decisive victories on the Napoleonic–Moltkean example. Their plans failed in 1914–18, but during the Second World War and in conventional conflicts such as the Gulf War there was a revival of Napoleonic strategy – feints, penetrations and envelopments by mobile forces covered and assisted by air power. Some analysts maintain that nuclear arsenals and missile-delivery systems have eliminated conventional wars between major powers. The issue remains unresolved. But whatever the outcome, as long as men follow the profession of arms, Napoleon's ability to inspire devotion and courage in the chaos of battle and his orchestration of great campaigns and battles will continue to exert a powerful attraction and will continue to be studied and perhaps admired.

Napoleon and his warmly dressed staff ride across the stricken field of Eylau.

CHAPTER ONE

The Transformation of War and the Emergence of Napoleon Bonaparte

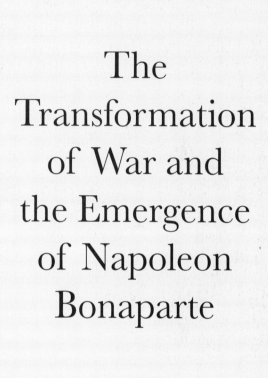
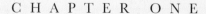

In September 1792 Austrian and Prussian units were pushing west through the Argonnes towards Paris. Here an allied advance guard emerging from a wooded defile is attacked by regular French line infantry still wearing its white uniforms. Note the general officers and the hussar in the foreground in dark blue coats, all with powdered hair and queues.

The Transformation of War and the Emergence of Napoleon Bonaparte

WHEN DARKNESS FELL ON 2 December 1805 the battle of Austerlitz came to a close. From his command post Emperor Napoleon watched the rout of the Austrian and Russian troops south of the Pratzen Heights. Further north the sounds of combat were fading as a Russian corps disengaged. When the emperor ordered a general ceasefire at 5 p.m. the enemy army had ceased to exist as an effective force and the will of his opponents to continue the war had been destroyed.

While Napoleon, then General Bonaparte, had made an impressive debut in Italy in 1796–7, the battle of Austerlitz was the triumphant finish to a campaign unprecedented in its sweep, speed and results. In little over three months, the emperor had projected his army from the Channel coast into the heart of central Europe, changed the balance of power in Germany, and effectively ended the Third Coalition against France. The swift and decisive operations awed contemporaries. Carl von Clausewitz, the great interpreter and philosopher of war, pronounced Napoleon the 'god of war', and the campaign set the pattern for the mobile, offensive and ruthless style of war, called Napoleonic.

MILITARY REFORMS BEFORE THE FRENCH REVOLUTION

The Napoleonic style was a synthesis of reforms and innovations suggested by others. His original contributions were few and mostly confined to the higher levels of warfare. But Napoleon systematized and elaborated reforms already under way and, with his personal genius, created the most effective army of its time, transforming the art of war itself. The arms and equipment as well as the troop types in his armies remained almost identical with those of Frederick the Great or even Marlborough. What had changed were the size of armies, their organization, command and control, and, above all, the ends for which they were employed, with the decisive, war-ending battle their paramount objective.

In the century before the French Revolution wars had become formal affairs, pursued with limited means for limited objectives by highly trained and brutally disciplined professional armies, commanded, especially in the higher ranks, by an aristocratic cousinage. Lacking ideological or national motivation, with limited agricultural, financial, industrial and chiefly manpower resources, operations were restricted in scope and intensity. Battles were avoided because heavy casualties, coupled with desertions, proved too costly for victors and vanquished alike. Wars commonly ended with the exhaustion of finances and manpower rather than with a decisive battle.

These constraints disappeared or were modified to a substantial degree in the latter decades of the eighteenth century. The shift from subsistence to surplus farming provided food which enabled Europe's population to roughly double. After Russia with 44 million, France, rising from 18 to 26 million by 1792, was the most populous country. The Habsburg Empire doubled its population from 9 to 18 million, roughly the same figure as Britain, while the population of all German states combined rose from 10 to 20 million. The agricultural economies of eastern and central Europe absorbed this increase in population, but in densely populated France it was only partially integrated, the remainder constituting a volatile urban mass – manpower for the armies of the Revolution and Napoleon. This demographic shift coincided with the early Industrial Revolution; output of iron and textiles greatly increased, and the early stages of mass production meant that arms and equipment could be supplied for the much-expanded military establishments. The expansion of industry, overseas trade and the improved means of administration and taxation provided better finances, especially in England where national income nearly doubled between 1712 and 1792.

The end of the Seven Years War in 1763 brought debates about improving war-fighting capabilities. France, where the humiliating defeats of the war had considerable impact, became the focus for military changes that impacted on Revolutionary and Napoleonic warfare. In the long run, the articulation of field armies into self-contained all-arms divisions appears as the single most important innovation. Marching along separate but parallel routes, these formations accelerated movement, reduced logistic problems and, able to fight alone or converge with others, increased strategic options. Suggested in 1759 by Marshal de Broglie, they were tested repeatedly during the following decades and permanently adopted after 1793. Divisions enabled the Revolutionary and Napoleonic armies to handle far greater numbers

EUROPE IN 1789

In 1789 France was compact, both Germany and Italy were divided into small states and principalities, while the Habsburg possessions included various lands from the Lower Rhine to Galicia and from Bohemia to northern Italy. Prussia was the largest German state, while Poland held substantial territories and the Ottoman Empire controlled the entire Balkan area.

Europe in 1789

boundary of the Holy Roman Empire

than had been previously possible. Command, control and co-ordination of several dispersed formations required an appropriate staff organization. In 1775 de Bourcet, a French staff officer, published schemes for using converging columns in mountain war, and in 1796 General Berthier, assigned as Bonaparte's chief of staff, wrote a detailed manual of staff procedure, later adopted throughout the French Army. Their smooth functioning staff system provided a great advantage for the French over their adversaries.

France also led in developing new infantry tactics. The long debate of 'line versus column' was resolved in favour of a combination put forward by de Guibert in 1772, proposing battalions in line and in columns, capable of rapidly shifting deployment according to the tactical situation, the *ordre mixte*. The essentials of this system were incorporated in the Regulations of 1791, the formal infantry doctrine of the armies of the Revolution and Napoleon, supplemented by renewed emphasis on skirmishing. There were improvements in artillery. Guns became more mobile and accurate, developments pioneered in Austria and Prussia, and introduced into the French service by de Gribeauval. While historians have made much of the supposed uniqueness of his range of field guns – 4-pounders, 8-pounders and 12-pounders – Austrian, Prussian and English artillery was nearly as hard-hitting and mobile as the French, and was often utilized when captured. The same was true of the standard flintlock muskets. The French model of 1772 with a 0.69-inch bore was not much superior to the weapons of other European powers, while the larger calibre 0.74-inch British musket inflicted the gravest injuries. Technology did not propel the transformation in war, though the capacity to produce the large quantity of weapons, ammunition and equipment required was crucial.

THE TRANSFORMATION OF WAR

When the wars of the Revolution began in 1792 many of the concepts and practices for more intensive and mobile war had already been discussed and, to a greater or lesser degree, introduced in France and other European states. But the great transformation of war did not result from improvements in weapons, tactics or army organization alone; its origins were political, social and ideological.

Even before the Revolution intellectuals had attacked professional armies as ineffective but expensive tools of royal absolutism, contrary to natural order and reason, and advocated their replacement with citizen soldiers. These ideas found support in the legislative bodies created after 1789 in France. As early as December 1789 a committee report to the Constituent Assembly asserted that 'every citizen must be a soldier and every soldier a citizen, or we shall never have a constitution'. While this radical proposal was rejected, the following year army reforms opened the officer corps to all classes, disbanded the foreign mercenary regiments, and supported the newly formed citizen National Guards. But as political and social turmoil continued, the regular and still royal army declined and when in the spring of 1792, driven by factional interests, France declared war on Austria and Sardinia and soon thereafter on Prussia, it became necessary to augment the weakened regulars with volunteers. By the spring of 1793 France, now a republic, was at war with Britain and Spain, joining

GRIBEAUVAL 12-POUNDER CANNON
Napoleon's preferred field piece, weighing 1,200 pounds. It was relatively mobile, with two trunnion positions, the forward for firing and the rear one, giving better balance, for travel. Gribeauval artillery was provided with an elevating screw mechanism and calibrated tangent rear sights, considered the most significant improvements in the design of ordnance during the last two hundred years of the smoothbore era.

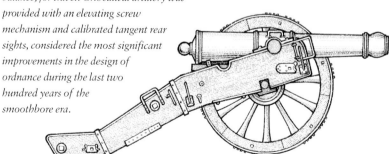

Austria, Prussia and Sardinia in the First Coalition. While facing armed counter-revolution in its western and southern regions, the country was invaded by converging foreign armies. Although the Allies, divided in their political objectives, wasted their opportunities, the situation appeared critical to the Republican government, the Convention, dominated by Jacobin ideologues.

To defend the Republic, the Committee of Public Safety, a strong executive body headed by Robespierre, instituted a quasi-dictatorship, the so-called 'Terror'. Robespierre did not favour a mass people's army and tried to rely on volunteers and the remaining regulars. But volunteering fell far short and on 23 August 1793, declaring 'the fatherland in danger', the Committee decreed the *levée en masse* which conscripted all national resources, human and material. French army numbers swelled while weapons, equipment and supplies were produced as a directed war economy. This was the real transformation of war, the result, as Clausewitz wrote, 'of the participation of the people in this great affair of state'.

Conscription worked. By the spring of 1794 over 750,000 men were available, adequately armed, trained and highly motivated. Their organization, training and overall strategy was directed by Carnot, formerly a captain of engineers, the 'organizer of victory', who from mid 1793 to the end of 1799 effectively supervised military affairs. Assisted by a small staff, the *bureau topographique*, he successfully amalgamated the diverse regular and volunteer elements into one national army, and directed offensive operations. Exploiting superior numbers, with losses easily replaced, and the Revolutionary faith in the bayonet, on 2 February 1794 he ordered troops 'to act in mass formation and take the offensive. Join action with the bayonet on every occasion. Give battle on a large scale and pursue the enemy until he is utterly destroyed.' Acting offensively in mass meant the attack column was often considered the characteristic Republican fighting method, but while the bayonet intimidated it was not actually the most effective weapon. By late 1794 the French adopted a flexible fighting system, its central aspect the quick interchange of line and column, with skirmishers and artillery according to circumstances.

French tactics were superior to the rigid linear deployments of their opponents, giving them qualified though not absolute combat superiority. The poorly led old-style armies, especially the Austrians and the Prussians, proved surprisingly tough and it was the bigger battalions that provided the decisive margin. Overall, the French usually were victorious when they fielded substantially superior numbers, but lost against equal or superior numbers. If Prussia and Austria had not retained major forces to assert rival claims in Poland the outcomes might have been different. The other members of the Coalition – Spain, Piedmont, Naples, the United Provinces and Portugal – played only a minor role, while the British contingent in Flanders was weak, the result of campaigns in the West Indies where nearly 100,000 men lost their lives, mainly to disease.

Much of the success of the Revolutionary forces was due to the rise of a new breed of young and aggressive senior commander. Before the Revolution nobles had constituted almost 90 per cent of the officer corps, but, loyal to the king rather than the Revolution, out of 9,578 officers on the establishment in 1789 some 5,500 had resigned or emigrated. The Republic had reason to mistrust the allegiance of those who remained; prominent generals like Lafayette and Dumouriez had defected. Moreover, with the army plunged into war and rapidly expanding, the government needed substantial numbers of officers and needed them quickly. Non-commissioned officers of the regular army provided the only manpower pool with some knowledge of tactics and battle experience. Together with a few junior officers, they provided new leaders, which at the height of the Terror were chosen as much for their ideological reliability as for their expertise. Officers were subject to political surveillance by all-powerful deputies in mission who, entrusted with absolute power by the Committee of Public Safety, enforced orders from Paris and punished failure, or non-compliance with their wishes, as treason. Seventeen generals were executed in 1793, another sixty-seven the following year. Even junior officers were not safe from the deputies' wrath.

Victory at any price became all-important and this propelled energetic officers into high command over the heads of senior but less daring men. Among them were Bonaparte, Davout, Jourdan, Hoche, Pichegru, Massena, Moreau, Ney and others, an array unmatched in talent and drive. By the end of 1794 the Republic's armies freed French territory from invaders and resumed the offensive into the Low Countries and Germany. The French armies moved faster than their enemies because they had abandoned much of the cumbersome supply impedimenta which slowed conventional armies. Adopted when the administrative machinery proved incapable of supplying the armies, the idea of letting the troops fend for themselves became standard practice in the armies of the Revolution and Napoleon, though basic rations, bread and wine, as well as ammunition, were still pre-stocked in depots.

Although, with revolts suppressed and the Revolution carried across the frontiers, the repressive Jacobin regime had been overthrown in mid summer 1794 and replaced by the more tolerant, and corrupt, Directoire, the new rulers had little incentive to make peace. Fearing that demobilization would bring social destabilization, they encouraged 'war nourishing war', with costs of the armies devolving largely on occupied countries, while commanders were expected to levy contributions to help keep France's finances afloat. In turn, the generals demanded freedom to formulate strategy and the removal of ideological controls. Dependent on the military to protect them against threats both from the right and the left, the Directors acquiesced.

In 1795 the French armies destroyed the First Coalition. Early in the year they had completed the conquest of the United Provinces and in April compelled evacuation of the British contingent. Prussia, at odds with Austria over Poland, concluded a peace treaty with France in the same month, and Spain left the war in July. Only Austria, France's most resilient enemy on land, remained at war, but, restrained by Prussian neutrality to the Upper Rhine and Italy, could not mount an offensive

In the face of a royalist insurrection, the Directoire entrusted its defence to Brigadier General Bonaparte. When on 5 October 1795 the Parisian mob attacked the Tuileries, Bonaparte, sending Captain Murat to collect some artillery, opened fire at point-blank range and with a 'whiff of grapeshot' crushed the revolt. A grateful Directoire promoted him to general of division.

challenge. For 1796 Carnot planned an ambitious two-pronged strategy to defeat Austria. Two armies in Germany would strike towards Vienna, supported by a subsidiary offensive from Italy. Chosen to command the Army of Italy was General Napoleon Bonaparte.

THE ASCENT OF NAPOLEON BONAPARTE

Napoleon Bonaparte liked to call himself a child of the Revolution, and indeed he was fortunate to have been born in 1769, the son of a minor Corsican noble family. Although his military talents amounted to genius it was the Revolution that offered him the opportunity to rise to high command in his twenties. Educated at royal military schools and commissioned into the artillery, he gained a reputation as a staunch Republican and established useful relations with influential politicians. In September 1793 chance, his republican reputation and his political connections placed him in charge of the artillery during the siege of Toulon, rising from captain to brigadier general in eight weeks.

In 1794 he served as chief of staff to French commanders in Italy, but after the overthrow of Robespierre found himself dismissed. Restored to duty with Carnot's staff he refused command of an infantry brigade engaged in counter-insurgency operations in the Vendée and resigned. But his political connections and luck held. When, on 5 October 1795, an armed uprising threatened the newly installed Directoire, General Bonaparte was put in charge of the 5,000 troops available to defend the government. Deploying artillery, he smashed the insurgents with the famous 'whiff of grapeshot'. The Directors thanked him with promotion to general of division, the highest rank in the Republican armies. Then, perhaps eager to get the charismatic general out of town, on 1 March 1796 they appointed him general-in-chief of the Army of Italy, a few near-mutinous and starving divisions in the Ligurian Alps.

This command became the crucial opportunity in Napoleon's meteoric ascent. In Italy he revealed the characteristics of his way of war, self-confident and mobile. He transformed what had been intended as a secondary theatre into a primary one, defeating the Austrians in Italy and in the following year compelling Vienna to make peace. Only three years later he was First Consul and in 1804, at the age of thirty-five, he crowned himself Emperor. Ahead were eleven years of great victories and, ultimately, disaster. It seems likely that events in France inevitably would have raised up a paramount military figure, but all we know of Napoleon's most competent rivals – Jourdan, Hoche, Moreau – suggests that if they had gained power, French political ambitions would have been more modest. If war had continued, the record of their campaigns suggests that they would have been defeated as often as not and that eventually exhaustion would have ended the conflict. But Napoleon prevailed and imposed his stamp on the wars, the Napoleonic Wars, from 1800 onwards.

ELEMENTS OF NAPOLEONIC WARFARE

Napoleon was not a great innovator but imposed his genius and personal leadership on the huge, largely conscript armies he inherited from the Revolution. He perfected their offensive, mobile and ruthless way of war, but though he often wrote and talked about the so-called principles of war he never enumerated them or wrote a comprehensive account of his own ideas.

Essentially he was a pragmatist, explaining that in war 'there are no precise or definite rules' and that 'the art of war is simple, everything is a matter of execution'. Even so, it is possible to deduce some constant elements from his campaigns, many already evident in Italy. Napoleon was convinced that unity of command was essential. 'In war,' he informed the Directoire, 'one bad general is better than two good ones.' He always fought offensively even when on the strategic defence – the destruction of the enemy's main field army, rather than the occupation of territory or the enemy's capital, his primary objective.

Strategic deployments were planned carefully. Even before hostilities opened efforts were made to shroud the emperor's intention. Newspapers were censored, borders closed, travellers detained. Swarms of light cavalry screened the army's advance and gathered intelligence about the location of the enemy. The self-contained corps marched along separate but parallel routes, deployed to cover the entire area of operations. When the main enemy body was located, Napoleon would close up deployment to bring his corps within supporting distance, adopting a loosely quadrilateral formation known as the *bataillon carré*. The first corps to contact the enemy would engage to pin him, while the others would hurry to its support. When concentration had been achieved Napoleon often disposed of superior numbers, but if this proved impossible he manoeuvred to gain local superiority at the decisive point. Still, several of his battles were won only by the fortuitous arrival of detached forces.

Success depended on tight security, good intelligence, precise staff work and, above all, great marching feats. Of these, the last two were difficult to achieve. In round numbers, 30,000 marching infantry required 8 kilometres of good road; 60 guns with their caissons took up 4 kilometres, and 6,000 cavalry, riding four abreast, needed about

7 kilometres. And strategic approach marches were long. In September–October 1805 several corps marched up to 300 kilometres in ten days; and in December Davout's corps, urgently summoned to Austerlitz, covered over 100 kilometres in two days; with an ample road network the *bataillon carré* formation was capable of rapid, large-scale movements.

In battle, as in his strategic approach, Napoleon always favoured the offensive. In all of his battles he stood only three times on the defensive – at Leipzig in 1813, and at La Rothière and Arcis in 1814 – and each time only after his initial attack had failed. Napoleon's battle plans – grand tactics – were similar to his strategic pattern. There were three major variants: the central position, the flanking envelopment and the frontal attack. The first he used when the enemy outnumbered his troops. He would seize the initiative, taking up a central position to divide the hostile forces. Then, while a portion of his troops engaged one part of the enemy force, he turned his main body against the other and defeated it. Finally, the main force would join the pinning force against the second opponent. In his second variant the flanking attack sometimes expanded into a full-scale envelopment, and involved one part of his army engaging the enemy front while a sudden attack crushed one of the flanks. If an envelopment was feasible there would be a holding action pinning the enemy, while the bulk of the army swept around him in forced marches – the famed *manoeuvre sur les derrières* – which compelled him either to surrender or to give battle with no satisfactory line of retreat. Finally, if time, terrain or the opponent's dispositions made either of these approaches impossible, there was the frontal attack, weakening the centre by threatening the flanks, and then launching the breakthrough force, the *masse de rupture*. Such attacks, however, required the use of combined arms, infantry, cavalry and artillery operating together with careful timing; they were costly and rarely successful.

A large part of Napoleon's success depended on his ability to inspire his subordinate commanders and his men. Courage and resolution were essential qualities for a general. Seniority counted for little and intellect alone even less. As he once said, 'I cannot abide promoting desk officers; I only like officers who make war.' If bravery and success were essential, favour also played a role, and he always retained a special regard for those who had served with him in Italy and Egypt.

Napoleon believed that personal leadership, coupled with appeals to pride, inspired men to fight, maintaining that 'the morale and opinion of the army are more than half the battle'. He understood that it was not, in the long run, the ideals of the nation, or of the Republic or the Revolution that motivated men. It was the army's romance of itself, expressed by symbols and legends. 'The military,' he is reported to have said, 'is a freemasonry and I am its Grand Master'; he reinforced these feelings both by personal rewards and recognition of corporate achievement. His personal charisma and his carefully fostered relations with his troops were most effective, even when luck had deserted him. Wellington believed that Napoleon's presence in battle was worth two corps.

THE ITALIAN CAMPAIGN: 1796–7

On 27 March 1796 General Bonaparte, accompanied by Berthier, his chief of staff until 1814, assumed command of the Army of Italy. On paper 63,100 strong, it actually numbered perhaps 37,000 combatants deployed on a 60-kilometre front in the Ligurian Alps, from Genoa to the north of Nice, facing 25,000 Piedmontese and 28,000 Austrians. With pay in arrears, rations poor, uniforms in tatters, many men lacking boots and some 1,000 muskets, the army was disaffected. With withdrawal into France unthinkable, Bonaparte resolved to break through into the rich Lombard plain and began to prepare an offensive. His decisiveness impressed his three senior generals – Augereau, Massena and Sérurier – already experienced commanders and unhappy to serve under an unproven leader. He also won over his soldiers by providing partial pay and promising to lead them into 'rich provinces and opulent towns … to find honour, glory and riches'. He opened his offensive on 10 April.

ITALIAN CAMPAIGNS 1796–7

The north Italian theatre of war where General Bonaparte conducted his first campaign, establishing his reputation.

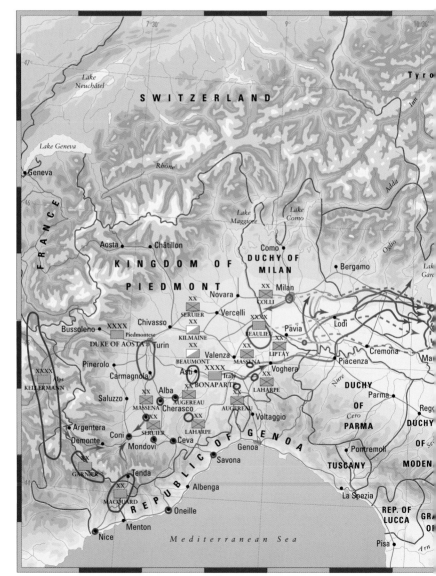

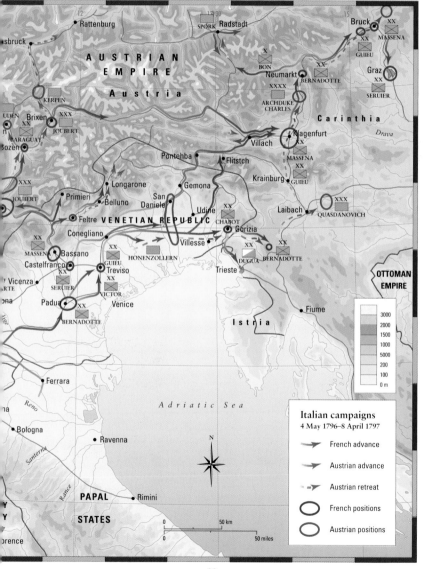

Italian campaigns
4 May 1796–8 April 1797

→ French advance
→ Austrian advance
⇢ Austrian retreat
◯ French positions
◯ Austrian positions

Montenotte Campaign
April 1796

→ French advance

⬭ Austrian-Piedmontese positions

Advance on Lodi
May 1796

→ French advance

⇢ Austrian retreat

⬭ French position

✕ French victory

The Austro-Piedmontese forces were deployed to block the several exits from the parallel valleys leading north and prevented by the mountain ridges from reinforcing their isolated detachments. This, Bonaparte recognized, presented an ideal situation for 'having larger forces at the point of attack', and in twelve days of almost continuous action, 10–22 April, striking always with superior numbers, he severed the Piedmontese from the Austrians. The Austrian Army was driven west and north across the Po river, while on 28 April Piedmont signed an armistice, surrendering three key fortresses and giving the French free use of its territory. Actual fighting had lasted but ten days. French troops had occasionally suffered minor setbacks and units had temporarily disintegrated when hungry, barefooted men entered a rich country, but in one month Bonaparte had reversed the situation existing when he took command. With his men well fed, paid in hard cash, their ammunition replenished, and their meagre artillery beefed up with captured pieces, he informed the Directoire that he expected shortly 'to be in the mountains of the Tyrol'. Meanwhile, he dispatched a substantial consignment of treasure to Paris.

With only 20,000 men remaining, the Austrian commander, General Beaulieu, planned to defend Milan by positioning himself in depth along the three northern tributaries of the Po, the river and neutral Piacenza protecting his flank. But Bonaparte, feinting with two divisions against the Austrian front, made a forced march of 115 kilometres in two days, along the south side of the Po and, not restrained by neutral status, crossed the river at Piacenza. This strategic

MONTENOTTE AND LODI

On 12 April 1796 Bonaparte struck against the junction of the Austrian and Piedmontese armies at Montenotte, then turned west against the Piedmontese while holding the Austrians. Driving back the Piedmontese in several battles, on 22 April his troops stormed the town of Mondovi, the entrance to the Piedmontese plain. The next day Piedmont asked for an armistice and made peace on 28 April. The Austrians withdrew east to cover Milan, but were outflanked when Bonaparte crossed the Po at Piacenza.

manoeuvre sur les derrières turned all of Beaulieu's river lines and compelled him to withdraw east across the Adda to the Mincio river, with a 7,000-strong rearguard covering the Adda bridge at Lodi.

On 10 May, assuming that he had located the main Austrian force, Bonaparte launched an attack column, supported by a 30-gun barrage, across the bridge. When the column stalled, Massena, Berthier and other senior officers rushed forward to urge the column on, while cavalry, fording the river further north, threatened the Austrian rear. Although in sober fact the assault across the bridge was not necessary and the majority of the Austrians got away, Lodi became a cornerstone of the Napoleonic legend. 'This battle,' he boasted the next day, 'is the most brilliant of the war,' while the Directoire, badly in need of good news, proclaimed 'immortal glory to the conquerors of Lodi!' Five days later Bonaparte occupied Milan, while Beaulieu retreated into the Tyrol and Venetia, leaving behind 15,000 men to defend Mantua, the key fortress.

At this point the Directoire, always in need of funds, insisted that he divert his force south to frighten Tuscany, Modena, Parma, the Papal States and Naples into neutrality, and more importantly to extract riches. The expedition yielded over 30 million francs and many art treasures, but it also gave the Austrians time to field a new army, 55,000 strong, commanded by General Würmser, 72 years old but an able and determined practitioner of the old-style war. From the end of July 1796 to mid January 1797 the war was dominated by two strategic factors. The first was that the French armies in Germany were contained and then defeated and driven back across the Rhine by the able Archduke Charles; the second was the tenacious defence of Mantua, a strong position dominating the gateway to Lombardy and the passage into the Tyrol and Venetia. As long as Mantua held out Bonaparte could not advance. With some 45,000 men, of whom 10,000 were tied up around Mantua and the remainder dispersed over 130 kilometres to cover the alpine passes, he had to stand on the defensive, scrambling to concentrate troops against four Austrian attempts to relieve the fortress. His position moreover was complicated by popular revolts flaring up in his rear.

*The Austrians renewed their attempts to relieve Mantua in late 1796,
advancing again along two converging axes of advance. On 15–17 November
Bonaparte gained one of his most celebrated victories at Arcola (Arcole),
a town near the confluence of the Adige and Alpone rivers. The outcome
of the battle was undecided until General Augerau's division managed to
cross the Adige at Albaredo on a pontoon bridge to push in the Austrian
line near Arcola.*

The mountain terrain compelled Würmser to utilize several axes.
During the first attack in July two columns advanced along opposite
shores of Lake Garda, the third came down the Brenta valley, supposed
to unite south of the lake to march on Mantua. The threat forced
Bonaparte to lift the siege in order to concentrate. Then, operating on
interior lines, he attacked the Austrian columns while they still were
separated, striking first at one and then the other. Performing
astonishing marching feats, Massena's division fought two

On 14 January 1797 Bonaparte defeats General Alvinczy and the main force of the last Austrian attempt to relieve Mantua at Rivoli.

engagements and one battle in one week, 29 July to 5 August, while covering 160 kilometres. He destroyed one column at Lonato on 4 August, which gave Bonaparte superior numbers, 35,000 against 25,000, to defeat Würmser at Castiglione the next day.

The second Austrian advance came in early September. Würmser and the main force moved down the Brenta valley while a second force under General Davidovich marched down the east side of Lake Garda. Again, Bonaparte used a *manoeuvre sur les derrières*. On 8 September he hit Würmser's rear at Bassano and pushed him into Mantua, adding 10,000 to a garrison already on short rations. There was little action in October. Attrition reduced the French to 24,000 fit for duty, while the Austrians, reinforced by troops from Germany, mustered for their third relief attempt. Commanded by General Alvinczy, the 30,000-strong main column moved west across the Venetian plain on Verona, while Davidovich with about 18,000 men came down the Adige valley. Alvinczy's advance began on 1 November and, opposed only by

Massena and Augereau, advanced to Caldiero, 15 kilometres west of Verona, and on 12 November repulsed a frontal attack by Bonaparte, who had taken command. Meanwhile Davidovich had pushed the weak French forces under Vaubois down the Adige, but stalled before the Rivoli plateau.

Bonaparte realized that his position would be desperate if the Austrians forced the Rivoli position and debouched in his rear; he therefore decided to cross the Adige to attack the Austrian left and rear. There followed the battle of Arcola, 15–17 November, three days of hard and confused combat amid marshes, dykes and rivulets. The outcome was still undecided when Alvinczy, with about a quarter of his

An important moment in the creation of the Napoleonic legend. On the second day of battle at Arcola, with the fighting at a stalemate, General Bonaparte seized a regimental colour to lead a grenadier assault column over a bridge.

force out of action, lost his nerve and withdrew. French losses were also severe; nine generals killed in action attested to the intensity of the fight. On 17 November Davidovich finally attacked Rivoli, but now Bonaparte could turn against him and by 19 November the Austrians were in full retreat. The year 1796 ended with the French controlling most of Italy, while the Austrians held Mantua and the alpine passes leading to their heartland, and Alvinczy, reinforced to 45,000, was preparing the fourth relief attempt against the Army of Italy, dispersed from Legnago to the western shore of Lake Garda.

He decided to attack in three columns. One force was to advance from Padua against Augereau around Legnago, the second from Vicenza against Massena at Verona, while he personally would lead the main column from Trent down the Adige valley against Joubert's division. The attack on Verona was repulsed on 13 January 1797, but the same day Alvinczy drove Joubert back to Rivoli. Recognizing the main threat, Bonaparte ordered Joubert to hold at all costs and directed a concentration at Rivoli. The next morning Bonaparte arrived on the battlefield to find that Joubert had managed to fight off several Austrian attempts to envelop his flanks. At 6 a.m. Massena's division, having marched 40 kilometres over ice-covered roads during the night, arrived together with other detachments, giving Bonaparte 23,000 men and 40 guns to fight 28,000 Austrians with 90 guns.

After heavy fighting the Austrians were first repulsed, and then routed. In all, the Austrians lost 12,000 men and much of their artillery. It was a clear defeat. That evening Massena left to force march his division 60 kilometres south to intercept an Austrian force trying to get to Mantua. He accomplished this and on 16 January destroyed it just outside the fortress. With hope for relief gone, the starving garrison capitulated on 2 February.

Once again delayed by diversions to the south to establish satellite republics and extract money, treasure and territory from the Papal States, Bonaparte, reinforced by two fresh divisions, resumed the strategic offensive into Austria. Sending Joubert to the Brenner Pass to cover his left flank, on 16 March he crossed the Tagliamento marching towards the Tarvis Pass. Austrian resistance collapsed. Even the Habsburgs' best general, Archduke Charles, urgently summoned from Germany, was unable to rally the troops. He advised Vienna that 'if this army is defeated, there is no salvation'. Only peace, he wrote, could save the monarchy. Neither then nor later would Charles stake everything on a decisive battle. His main objective always was to preserve the army he considered the main guarantor of the dynasty.

Bonaparte's position was in fact vulnerable. Joubert had run into staunch local resistance in the Tyrol, there was a rising in Venetia and his line of communications was tenuous. Still, he pushed on to Leoben in Styria while Massena was at Bruck, 160 kilometres from Vienna. On 7 April the Austrians asked for a five-day suspension – twice renewed – while Bonaparte, acting alone, negotiated an armistice that was signed on 18 April. The two armies disengaged. The French withdrew beyond the Isonzo river, the Austrians regrouped west of Vienna.

After further negotiations, on 17 October, the Peace of Campo Formio was signed. Austria ceded Belgium and Lombardy, accepted French rule on the left bank of the Rhine, and recognized the French satellite republics in Italy as well as French control of Venetian possessions in the Adriatic – a foothold in the eastern Mediterranean. In return, the Habsburgs received the Venetian mainland, including Venice, and its fleet. Also, the treaty called for a congress to be held at Rastatt to discuss compensation for German princes for losses on the left bank of the Rhine, giving France further scope in Germany.

In his first command Bonaparte had changed the face of Europe and become one of the leading generals of the Republic with a substantial following in the army. Italy and the Army of Italy would always hold a special place in his heart and he would never forget his first campaign and the officers and men of that small, highly motivated army.

CHAPTER TWO

Egypt, the Second Coalition and the Grande Armée

Napoleon reorganized his cavalry which was in poor condition after the Revolutionary Wars. Perhaps the most famed of his 'heavy' cavalry were the regiments of Cuirassiers, heavy men on heavy horses, wearing steel breast and backplate armour and steel helmets, wielding heavy straight swords. Considered élite troops, they justified the emperor's expectations in many battles, and despite their expense he raised additional Cuirassier regiments. The picture here is of Lieutenant Charles Legrand, 12th Cuirassier Regiment, killed on 2 May 1808 in Madrid.

Egypt, the Second Coalition and the Grande Armée

THE EGYPTIAN INTERLUDE

After Campo Formio, except for Portugal, England stood alone – unable to confront France on land, but keeping up her naval blockade while seeking new continental allies. Meanwhile, Bonaparte's return as an acclaimed conquering hero frightened the weak Directoire. Refusing command of an army to invade England early in 1798, he proposed instead seizing Egypt as a base from which to attack Britain's trade and possessions in India. The moment seemed opportune. After Spain had allied herself with France, the British fleet had withdrawn from the Mediterranean in December 1796, while in Egypt the Mamelukes, a warrior caste, had replaced Turkish rule. If the expedition could be represented as a move to restore the position of the Ottoman court at Constantinople – the sublime Porte – then the sultan might assent to French invasion and Egypt become a French base in the eastern Mediterranean.

The Directoire felt the potential benefits were worth risking a small army, and undoubtedly was pleased to have found distant employment for a politically ambitious general. But the enterprise was based on false assumptions. The Royal Navy had returned to the Mediterranean in May 1798 and without secure sea communications the Egyptian venture had no chance of lasting success. None the less, that same month, the Army of the Orient, 35,000 strong, sailed from Toulon and other ports. The British knew of its departure, but were uncertain of its destination.

Evading the British fleet, and seizing Malta from the Knights of St John on its way, the expedition arrived off Alexandria on 1 July. After taking the city Napoleon moved on Cairo: 15,000 men marched across the desert, another 10,000 were shipped upriver by barge. On 17 July the reunited army brushed aside a Mameluke force at Shubra Khit and on 21 July encountered the main host – 6,000 mounted Mamelukes and

54,000 local levies – at the battle of the Pyramids, some 3 kilometres north-west of Cairo. The battle was one-sided. Mameluke charges against the large division squares made no impression and the local levies took almost no part in the action. Impressed by the Mamelukes' bravery, Bonaparte recruited some for his bodyguard.

The French entered Cairo on 22 July, but on 1 August Nelson destroyed their fleet in Aboukir Bay, marooning the army. Bonaparte expected the government to ship reinforcements and that diplomacy would keep Turkey neutral. But, enraged by the seizure of Malta, Tsar Paul I declared war, and, yielding to Russian and English pressure, Sultan Selim I decreed Holy War against the infidels.

Before the battle of the Pyramids, 21 July 1798, Bonaparte reputedly told his Army of the Orient that 'forty centuries of history look down on you'. When this battle was over French casualties were twenty-nine dead and about two hundred wounded; the Mamelukes had lost thousands, rich plunder for the French soldiers.

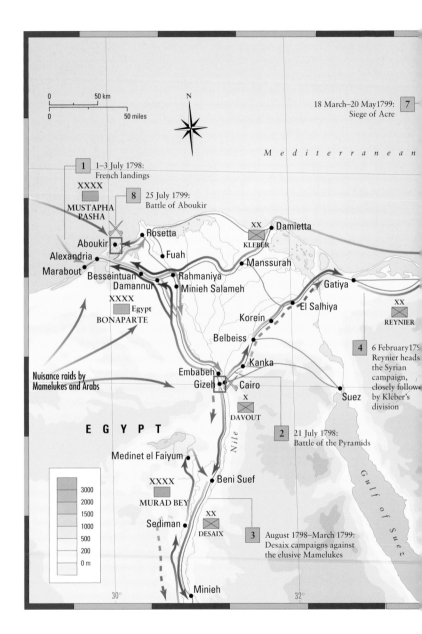

0 ⊢——⊣ **50 km**
0 ⊢——⊣ **50 miles**

N

18 March–20 May 1799: **7**
Siege of Acre

M e d i t e r r a n e a n

1 1–3 July 1798:
French landings

XXXX

**MUSTAPHA
PASHA**

8 25 July 1799:
Battle of Aboukir

Rosetta

XX Damietta

Aboukir

KLÉBER

Alexandria
Fuah

Marabout
Manssurah

Besseintuan
Rahmaniya

Damannur
Minieh Salameh

XXXX
Egypt
BONAPARTE

Gatiya

El Salhiya

Korein

XX
REYNIER

Belbeiss

4 6 February 179
Reynier heads
the Syrian
campaign,
closely follow
by Kléber's
division

Kanka

Nuisance raids by
Mamelukes and Arabs

Embabeh

Gizeh
Cairo

Suez

X
DAVOUT

2 21 July 1798:
Battle of the Pyramids

E G Y P T

Nile

Medinet el Faiyum

Beni Suef

XXXX
MURAD BEY

XX
DESAIX

Sediman

3 August 1798–March 1799:
Desaix campaigns against
the elusive Mamelukes

Gulf of Suez

3000
2000
1500
1000
500
200
0 m

Minieh

30°
32°

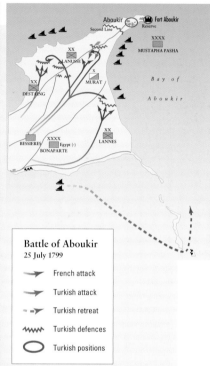

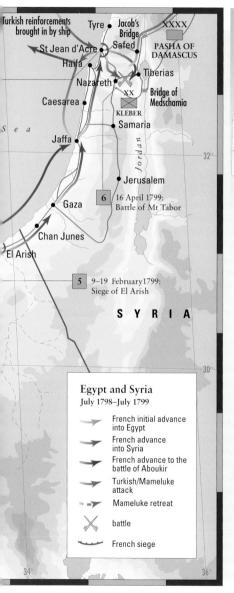

Battle of Aboukir
25 July 1799

- French attack
- Turkish attack
- Turkish retreat
- Turkish defences
- Turkish positions

Egypt and Syria
July 1798–July 1799

- French initial advance into Egypt
- French advance into Syria
- French advance to the battle of Aboukir
- Turkish/Mameluke attack
- Mameluke retreat
- battle
- French siege

THE BATTLE OF ABOUKIR, 25 JULY 1799

After his return from the abortive expedition into Palestine and Syria, Bonaparte was faced with the Turkish army of Rhodes which had landed at Aboukir on 11 July and taken up defensive positions. On 25 July, with Murat leading a charge across the earthworks, Bonaparte smashed the Turks.

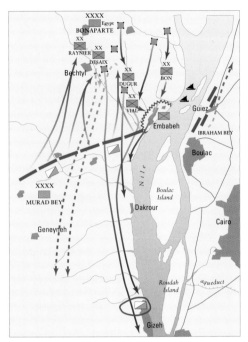

Battle of the Pyramids
21 July 1798

→ French attack

→ Mameluke attack

- -→ Mameluke retreat

᠕᠕᠕ Mameluke defences

◯ Mameluke positions

THE BATTLE OF THE
PYRAMIDS 1798
*Having occupied Lower Egypt, on
21 July 1798 Bonaparte marched
on Cairo where his army, formed
into five large rectangles, defeated
the Mameluke cavalry of Murad
Bey in the battle of the Pyramids.
Sheltered behind the ramparts of
Embabe, the local levies took no
part in the fighting but withdrew
across the Nile.*

While Bonaparte installed a local administration, General Desaix pursued remaining Mameluke forces and on 7 October scattered them at Sediman, 80 kilometres south-west of Cairo. The French controlled only a few major cities; the countryside was never pacified and even in Cairo there was a sudden uprising on 21 October that was sternly suppressed. Despite a worsening situation, amid a hostile population, cut off from support and losing strength daily, Bonaparte decided to pre-empt a Turkish attack on Egypt by invading Syria. Suggestions that he envisioned a march on Constantinople, or even India, must be discounted – his force was barely adequate to control Egypt and repel the approaching Turks.

Leaving 5,000 to garrison Cairo, while Desaix with 4,000 pacified Upper Egypt, the 13,000-strong army left on 6 February 1799, its siege-train following by sea, its advance delayed when the fort at El Arish resisted for eleven days. Moving up the coast to Jaffa, he stormed the port on 7 March, killing some 2,000 defenders and ordering 2,500 prisoners to be shot. While exploited by British propaganda and condemned by later historians, Bonaparte had little choice: he could not spare men to guard prisoners. The fact that the Turks had tortured captured French soldiers contributed to his decision.

He reached his next objective, Acre – an ancient Crusader stronghold – on 17 March. Defended by units of the Ottoman New Model Army, the Nizam I Jedid, assisted by British naval gunners, Acre stopped Bonaparte. His siege-train captured by a British squadron, he launched seven direct assaults, all repulsed. Although, on 16 April, General Kleber handily defeated a Turkish relief effort, this did not assist the siege. With plague decimating his ranks and a Turkish army embarking on Rhodes for Egypt, Bonaparte tried a last assault on 10 May and retreated ten days later proclaiming his objectives achieved.

By this time he realized that the venture was lost and knew of the Directoire's setbacks against the Second Coalition – Britain, Russia, Turkey, Naples, Portugal and, above all, Austria, which had re-entered the war in March 1799. Bonaparte decided to quit Egypt. As early as 21 June he had secretly readied two frigates and alerted some key officers and scientists to accompany him. But he still had one more victory. On 11 July the Turks, 18,000 strong, had landed at Aboukir. Bonaparte rapidly concentrated 10,000 men and smashed them on 25 July.

On 22 August, accompanied by only three senior generals – Berthier, Lannes and Murat – and a handful of other officers including Andréossy, Marmont and Bessières, members of his household and 200 men of the Guides, he sailed for France. Left behind was General Kleber and a dwindling and disillusioned army. On 9 October Bonaparte landed on French soil and arrived in Paris a week later. With news of his victory at Aboukir preceding him, he was fêted and attracted the attention and the support of a faction eager to overthrow the Directoire. Back in Egypt, despite unrest and British–Turkish pressure, Kleber, and after his assassination General Menou, managed to hold out until 1801. A spectacular British assault landing at Aboukir followed and the French were defeated in the field. The remaining troops capitulated in September and were repatriated.

With Bonaparte already preparing to leave Egypt, the battle of Aboukir, 25 July 1799, was a short, sharp frontal action in which a hastily collected French force defeated a Turkish expedition, the Army of Rhodes, that had landed near Alexandria. With Murat's cavalry overrunning the Turkish defences, the enemy routed and sustained heavy casualties while fleeing back to the ships. Another part of the enemy took refuge in Aboukir Castle, which they held until 2 August.

THE STRATEGIC PICTURE IN 1799

By the time Menou capitulated the Directoire was over, replaced in November 1799 by a new regime, the three-man Consulate. Bonaparte, one of the consuls, then outwitted his colleagues and on 25 December, with substantial military backing, became First Consul, head of the government. His first priority was to recover territory lost to the Second Coalition. In 1799 Austrian and Russian armies had gained victories in Germany and Italy. In Germany Archduke Charles had driven the French back to the Rhine; in Italy Austro-Russian forces had cleared most of the Peninsula. By the end of the year, however, fortunes began to turn. In September General Soult's victory at Zurich regained control of the strategic north–south passes, while, unable to agree on strategy and war aims, the Second Coalition collapsed. From Switzerland the Russians withdrew into Germany and a joint Anglo-Russian expedition into northern Holland also failed. The volatile Tsar Paul I ordered his troops home and left the Coalition early in 1800.

Thus, when Bonaparte took power, the Republic had recovered Switzerland, but Italy was lost and its lodgement in southern Germany threatened. Also that winter insurrections flared up again in western France, while the Allies – Spain, the Netherlands and Switzerland – were unenthusiastic. Taking control, the First Consul launched an impressive series of internal administrative, constitutional and military improvements. He militarized artillery drivers and reorganized the Consular Guard; but the most important measure was the establishment of army corps – multi-divisional formations, used experimentally during the 1790s, both in Italy and on the Rhine. Their formal introduction dated to 1 March 1800 when Bonaparte directed General Moreau to divide his Army of the Rhine into four corps. Corps became the major manoeuvre element of Napoleonic armies, comprising two or more infantry divisions, a division or brigade of light cavalry, a number of batteries, detachments of engineers and other service troops. Commanded by a senior general, later a marshal, corps were capable of independent operations.

THE MARENGO CAMPAIGN: PREPARATIONS

Aware that the French people desired peace, Bonaparte made overtures to England and Austria, though he insisted on keeping Belgium, Piedmont and Genoa as parts of France, with Switzerland and Holland as French satellites. The Second Coalition rejected his terms. The First Consul had expected as much and already, in January 1800, had ordered Berthier to assemble an Army of Reserve – three infantry divisions, a cavalry brigade and the Consular Guard – around Dijon, close to the alpine passes. French control of Switzerland meant that the

Army of Reserve could reinforce either Moreau's Army of the Rhine or Massena's Army of Italy. With over 120,000 men, the Army of the Rhine was France's strongest army; the Army of Italy dispersed in the Maritime Alps and on the Ligurian coast numbered only 36,000.

As always, Austria was the principal adversary. General Kray commanded 108,500 men along the Upper Rhine and Danube, while General Mélas had about 93,000 in Italy. Initially, Bonaparte considered the Austrian army between the Upper Rhine and Danube as the paramount strategic objective. His intent was for Moreau to pin Kray with one corps in the Black Forest, while the combined Armies of the Rhine and the Reserve swung through Switzerland into the rear of the opponent. This would result in his destruction and open the road to Vienna. If necessary, the Army of Reserve could pivot through Switzerland into Mélas's rear to eliminate remaining Austrian forces.

But Moreau was averse to Bonaparte's directions, asserting that the proposed strategy was too risky. The First Consul lacked power to replace the recalcitrant general. Moreau was among the greatest generals of the Republic and his Army of the Rhine as loyal to him as the Army of Italy was to Bonaparte. Any attempt to relieve him might have precipitated a major mutiny. Therefore Bonaparte instructed Moreau to proceed with his frontal offensive, but requested that he detach a corps to the St Gotthard Pass to reinforce the Army of Reserve's strike into the rear of the Austrians in Italy.

Austrian offensive plans assumed that the French were weak in Germany and, as Bonaparte had hoped, discounted the Army of Reserve. Mélas was to smash Massena, then advance through the Maritime Alps into southern France to be joined by a British expeditionary force assembling on Minorca. This would draw French troops from the Rhine front, enabling Kray to penetrate through Alsace into France. On 6 April Mélas hit Massena's command and split it. Massena was besieged in Genoa with only four weeks' rations for his 10,000 men; General Suchet, with 18,000, was pushed west beyond the River Var. In Germany Moreau hesitated and only attacked in late

April. On 3 and 6 May he defeated Kray at Stockach and Moskirch and drove him into a fortified camp at Ulm, removing a potential threat to Bonaparte's rear. Moreau's tardiness had delayed Bonaparte's offensive and instead of the promised corps he merely detached a division to the St Gotthard Pass. But finally Bonaparte was able to execute his great strategic *manoeuvre sur les derrières*. Time had become of the essence while Massena still pinned 21,000 Austrians and Suchet another 30,000. The First Consul took a gamble. Victory would secure his position, though a major defeat might unseat him and end the consular regime.

MARENGO AND HOHENLINDEN

In the second week of May Bonaparte, who had remained in Paris to prod Moreau into action, arrived at the headquarters of the Army of Reserve, ostensibly an adviser because the new constitution did not allow the First Consul to hold command. He planned to traverse the Alps through five different passes. The easiest passage from Geneva was the Little St Bernard Pass, but Bonaparte rejected this approach because it would need a larger supply train than the more difficult Great St Bernard route which

Crossing the Alps through the Great St Bernard Pass in May 1800 with the main column of the Armée de Réserve. *Undertaken unusually early in the year, the passage required special measures to be taken to bring the guns to the head of the pass with cannons disassembled and barrels pulled on special sledges by teams of soldiers.*

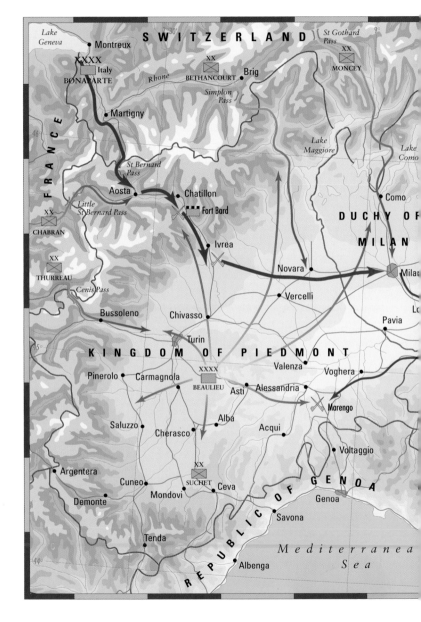

Crossing the Alps
15 May – 14 June 1800

→ French advance

→ Austrian advance

⚔ site of battle

▪▪▪ fort

0   20 km

0   20 miles

ergamo **V E N E T I A N**

R E P U B L I C
Brescia   *Lake Garda*

Mantua

Piacenza

DUCHY Parma

OF
Cero   Reggio

PARMA

DUCHY

OF *Sechia*
Pontremoli

MODENA

La Spezia   **REP. OF LUCCA**

was closer to the depots established on Lake Geneva. Careful arrangements were made to move the main body through this 40-kilometre pass, while, to confuse Mélas, small detachments would come over the four remaining passes. On 14 May Bonaparte ordered the advance guard under Lannes to proceed, and by 16 May it had descended as far as Aosta. Six days later the army crossed over the pass, though Fort Aosta held up passage of artillery.

Leaving behind a detachment to invest the fort, Bonaparte proceeded with only six small guns. Although aware of Massena's desperate situation in Genoa, Bonaparte did not march to relieve it. Instead, he swung eastwards to cut Austrian communications and capture Milan and its arsenal on 2 June. Here he waited for the arrival of the corps promised by Moreau, in the event only 11,000 men. Meanwhile, Massena had capitulated on 4 June. He had carried

OPERATIONS IN NORTH-WESTERN ITALY,
APRIL TO JUNE 1800

With Massena and Suchet grimly hanging on in the west, Bonaparte's handling of the crossing over the Alps, followed by his unexpected turn towards Milan, compromised Austrian communications. This confused their command, leading to their concentration near Alessandria. The battle of Marengo followed on 14 June.

out his mission until his men had almost starved to death and then delayed surrender for another two days while negotiating excellent terms. Mélas occupied Genoa, but, now aware of the Army of Reserve in his rear, ordered a general concentration at Alessandria, about halfway between Turin and Genoa. By 10 June he had assembled 32,000 men and 100 guns. From Alessandria he could either retreat into Genoa where he would have British naval support, or he could fight for northern Italy.

The Austrian concentration induced Bonaparte to advance west through Montebello, where Lannes won a sharp engagement on 9 June, and late on 13 June he crossed the Scrivia river into the plain east of Alessandria on the far side of the Bormida river. His army numbered about 31,500 men with forty guns. Among the commanders present was Desaix, returned from Egypt on the First Consul's express orders. Convinced that Mélas wished to escape, Bonaparte divided his army and detached three divisions, including two under Desaix, to block likely Austrian escape routes.

Not expecting trouble, the remainder bivouacked for the night around the small village of Marengo. When Mélas attacked on 14 June a surprised Bonaparte found himself with only 22,000 men and 20 guns facing a far superior enemy supported by 100 cannon. Although the attack developed slowly and there were some defensive positions on the plain, by noon massive Austrian infantry assaults forced the French back. Bonaparte committed his last reserve – the Consular Guard – but, heavily outnumbered and low on ammunition, the battle seemed lost. Desperate messages went out recalling detached formations, while, convinced that the day was won, Mélas handed over command to a subordinate. But the French hung on grimly. At about noon Desaix returned with one division and, assisted by Marmont who scraped up eighteen guns to provide close fire support, and a charge by the surviving cavalry, the counter-attack stampeded the victorious but fatigued enemy. The unexpected blow by almost fresh troops converted defeat into victory. As Napoleon later commented, 'The fate of a battle is a single moment ... the decisive moment arrives, the moral spark is kindled and

Although the defeat at Marengo had forced the Austrians to withdraw from Italy, they continued to hold Germany. When, after an armistice, hostilities reopened in the winter of 1800, an Austrian army under the inexperienced Archduke John was ambushed in the forest of Hohenlinden, east of Munich, on 3 December. Austria now signed an armistice and negotiations towards a peace settlement were begun.

the smallest reserve force settles the issue.' And he had learned from his close call. Never again would he disperse his main force in the face of the enemy, and whenever possible he would retain a strong reserve.

The Marengo campaign was a strategic masterpiece, but the conduct of the battle was far from brilliant and the official account would be rewritten several times to enhance Napoleon's reputation. Meanwhile, at the cost of 6,000 casualties, including Desaix who was shot leading the assault, the First Consul had his victory. Austrian casualties equalled the French, though they also lost 8,000 prisoners and 40 cannons. Mélas was stunned and the next day signed an armistice evacuating all of Lombardy up to the Mincio river, halting all fighting until Vienna had responded to a peace proposal. Even so, the Austrian army was not destroyed. Re-forming behind the Mincio it still numbered some 55,000 men and 300 guns. In Germany Moreau advanced to Munich, and in July concluded an armistice that lasted until November.

One more victory was needed to finish the Second Coalition. This Moreau provided when the fighting resumed. In Germany, Archduke Charles not only refused to accept command, but he also advised that Austria should make peace while there was still an army. But Vienna decided to try once more. With the inexperienced 18-year-old Archduke John in command, hostilities recommenced on 22 November with an attempt to crush Moreau's left flank and cut his communications. Moreau ambushed the Austrian columns on 2 December at Hohenlinden, 33 kilometres east of Munich, and routed them. This disaster convinced Austria to sign an armistice on 25 December, which was followed on 9 February 1801 by the Peace of Lunéville, confirming the terms of Campo Formio.

Britain continued the conflict alone, her position complicated when Tsar Paul I organized a league of northern states – Russia, Sweden, Denmark and Prussia – threatening her naval supplies. Britain responded with an attack on Copenhagen, destroying major elements of the Danish fleet. Soon thereafter, Paul was murdered in a palace revolt and his successor Alexander I dismantled the league. Even so, England was weary of war, while Bonaparte wished to consolidate his regime. As a result, after prolonged haggling, the Treaty of Amiens was signed on 27 March 1802.

NAPOLEON AND HIS GRANDE ARMÉE

Allied victories during the War of the Second Coalition indicated that they could still compete with the French. Neither Marengo nor Hohenlinden were proof of a systemic inferiority to the French, though the changes in strategy, operations and organization, introduced by the Revolution and Bonaparte, pointed to a new style of warfare. But it would take time for the new model to take hold and for Napoleon, as he styled himself following his self-elevation to Emperor of the French and King of Italy in 1804, effectively to take control of the entire French military establishment.

Under the Republic and the Directoire there had emerged serious rivalries and ill-feeling between the various armies which had developed separate styles and cultures of their own. Especially dangerous was the bad blood between Moreau's old Army of the Rhine and the troops who had served with Bonaparte in Italy and Egypt; this lingered on for many years among senior officers. In 1811 Napoleon observed that Marmont would make an excellent choice to replace Ney who had clashed with Massena in Spain, because 'both are from the same family; they are of the Army of Italy, while Ney is from a foreign army [the Army of the Rhine]'. The First Consul's main priority was to consolidate his authority. Moreau remained a bitter rival and his troops sullen. Therefore, soon after the Treaty of Amiens, substantial elements of these troops were shipped to San Domingo, while Moreau, enmeshed in a royalist intrigue, was imprisoned and sent into exile after the establishment of the Empire.

In 1802 Napoleon created his military instrument, the Grande Armée designating the principal force of French and allied troops operating under the emperor's command. When, on 18 May 1803, Britain declared war on France, he activated the Army of the Ocean Coasts along the Channel and the North Sea. For the first and only time troops received systematic training, practised new tactics and received new equipment. Incompetent officers were weeded out, deserving officers promoted and higher formations organized. But problems remained. Cavalry was poorly mounted and so short of horses that one dragoon division had to fight dismounted. Horse shortages also affected transport and artillery. Transport remained inadequate and the artillery, despite Napoleon's dictum that 'it is with cannon that one makes war', was relatively weak. The original Grande Armée had only two pieces for every thousand men, and the target of five per thousand men was never achieved even when captured guns were incorporated into its batteries. If Napoleon's artillery remained numerically inferior to that of his opponents, he transformed it from a support to an offensive arm, concentrating its weight at decisive points.

Three years of hard training had overcome the legacy of neglect left by the Directoire, and when he went to war in 1805 Napoleon could justly claim that his Grande Armée was the finest army in Europe. That year its order of battle comprised seven corps, to which one allied corps was added. Moreover, there were three major formations Napoleon kept under his own control: the Army Cavalry Reserve of six heavy mounted divisions; the Army Artillery Reserve with almost a quarter of available guns; and finally the élite Imperial Guard which expanded at a fast rate.

In 1808 considerable parts of the Grande Armée were shifted to Spain, and Napoleon hastily formed a new main force – the Army of Germany – in 1809. In 1812, once again designated as the Grande Armée, it invaded Russia. Following the Russian disaster, the Grande Armée was hastily reconstituted in 1813 and came to its end when Napoleon abdicated in April 1814. During his last campaign in 1815 the units under his command were designated as the Armée du Nord.

COMMAND, CONTROL AND ADMINISTRATION OF THE GRANDE ARMÉE

Napoleon practised extreme centralization of authority. As ruler of France and commander-in-chief he required a substantial staff apparatus. Over time, Imperial Headquarters with its subsidiary staffs, agencies, escorts and attached personnel became large and unwieldy, but his personal staff – the *Maison* – remained small. It included Berthier, his chief of staff, Bacler d'Albe, his indispensable topographical officer, as well as officers responsible for daily reports and briefings, correspondence and situation maps. In addition there was a pool of trusted senior aides who would be sent on special tasks, acting 'in the Name of the Emperor'. The General Staff of the Grande Armée, also headed by Berthier, was responsible for transmitting routine orders, and co-ordinating movements, intelligence, military finances, justice and medical services. Finally, and never functioning smoothly, was the staff of the Commissary General.

The *Maison* enabled Napoleon to control large forces, but it never became the brain of the army. The emperor was his own operations officer and made all decisions. As Berthier put it: 'The Emperor needs neither advice nor plans of campaign. No one knows his thoughts and our duty is to obey.' Yet, if his role generally was passive, Berthier was more than just a titular chief of staff and few could have matched his planning for passing 150,000 troops across the Danube at Wagram.

Combining the powers of chief of state and supreme commander had distinct advantages for strategic planning. As head of state Napoleon was able to combine diplomacy and strategy to support each other and to set clear political and military objectives. Yet the system had serious limitations. The forces he commanded grew from 50,000 to well over 400,000 men, yet Napoleon maintained his personal control. But when his armies operated in widely separated theatres of war, or over an extended front, his attempts to maintain strategic control failed.

Ramshackle logistics remained a shortcoming. Despite his pronouncement that 'an army marches on its stomach', he remained essentially an improviser. To be sure, he repeatedly laid down huge magazines, such as in 1800, 1807 and again 1812, but the problem of bringing these supplies forward remained. In 1807, to improve transport arrangements which were still handled by civilian contractors, he formed nine transport battalions and introduced a network of military staging areas. But he never allocated sufficient manpower to these needs and, with his strategy geared to rapid movements, large wagon trains, even if they had existed, could not have kept pace. As it was, troops had to maintain themselves. This was practical in rich areas and when the units were spread out, but when concentrated it did not work well, but in poor countries – Poland, Spain or Russia – the practice could produce calamities. Moreover, foraging and requisitioning aroused local resentment and adversely affected discipline, something already experienced in 1796; but Napoleon could never break with the system and even argued that 'an army of 20,000 can subsist even in a desert'. He was wrong. The price paid for ruthless requisitioning was resentment, escalating into rebellions, some repressed promptly but others, such as the guerrilla war in Spain, becoming a running sore.

Napoleonic strategy aimed to concentrate superior forces against the enemy and in many, though by no means all, of his battles his forces outnumbered those of his opponents. This hardly detracts from Napoleon's generalship. Achieving numerical superiority required the ability to calculate accurately time, space and terrain, as well as meticulous staff work – one of the major advantages he enjoyed over his adversaries – supplemented by the outstanding marching capabilities of his troops.

NAPOLEON'S SOLDIERS: OFFICERS AND MEN

Corps were usually commanded by one of the marshals, a rank created by Napoleon in 1804. Altogether he created twenty-six marshals – eighteen in 1804, the remainder between 1807 and 1815. The original appointments included some deserving Revolutionary generals: Sérurier, Perignon, Lefebvre and Kellermann, while a fifth went to Brune, who enjoyed excellent Republican connections. Ney and Mortier represented the famous Army of the Sambre and Meuse, but most initial promotions went to comrades from Italy and Egypt – Augereau, Berthier, Bessières, Davout, Lannes, Marmont, Massena and Murat. Bernadotte may have been appointed because he had married the sister of Napoleon's elder brother's wife, yet he was the least reliable.

The marshals hailed from diverse social backgrounds, ten had served in the ranks of the royal army, and all were brave and had seen much active service. But only Davout, Massena and, perhaps, Suchet had the greater measure of imaginative intellect required for independent command at the higher formation level. The emperor, however, failed to raise the professional competence of his senior officers, and also did not establish an effective hierarchy among them, so that they often failed to co-operate with each other.

Marshals, generals and combat officers generally shared the supreme disregard for danger cultivated in the army. French officer casualties were the highest by far among all combatants. Overall, the Imperial Army suffered about 50,000 officer casualties, with 15,000 killed between 1805 and 1815, including close to 900 generals. Proportionally, losses of English, Austrian, Prussian and Russian senior officers were much lower. This follow-me type of leadership, expected by French troops, contributed to the combat effectiveness of Napoleon's armies.

At the intermediate and lower levels the Napoleonic officer corps retained a hard core of veterans from the royal and Revolutionary armies, and of the 5,000 officers in the first Grande Armée nearly all had combat experience. On average, the regimental officers were older than generals and had served in the king's army. As colonels, majors and captains they remained the mainstay of Napoleon's officer corps. Entrance into the corps was possible by a number of avenues: spot promotion on the battlefield, through the military schools and by transfer from foreign regiments taken into the French service. The military schools, especially the *École speciale militaire* at Saint Cyr, produced nearly 5,000 officers, while spot promotions, especially after 1809 when losses became heavy, accounted for between a quarter and one-fifth of all Napoleonic officers. Though few rankers promoted on the battlefield rose beyond the grade of captain, opportunities were far greater than in any other contemporary army and served as a potent morale booster.

Under Napoleon recruitment continued to follow the Jourdan Law of 1798. In practice, the number actually conscripted was not excessive – one and a half million between 1800 and 1815. This was less than seven per cent of the population of France proper, and, with the Empire steadily expanding and annexed areas subject to conscription, the percentage was even lower. Conscription was for five years; exemptions could be purchased, but the continued wars after 1805 blocked discharges. In 1804 the army still had some 170,000 men in its ranks, enlisted or conscripted between 1793 and 1799, their service far from over.

Morale was maintained by positive motivation, opportunities for promotion and, above all, unit cohesion as regiments developed corporate pride. Between 1806 and 1810 – the glory years – desertion rates dropped below three per cent. Napoleon's infantry received little formal training and a soldier was expected to pick up what he needed on the march to his unit and from his more experienced fellow soldiers. This system worked fairly well as long as experienced role models were available, but it deteriorated after 1809 and never worked well for the cavalry or the artillery.

Within the Grande Armée, the Imperial Guard – the *corps d'élite*, formally established in 1804 – occupied a special place. Its origins went back to the Guides that had escorted Bonaparte in Italy and Egypt, the Guard of the Directoire and the Consular Guard. At the outset the Imperial Guard numbered 5,000 infantry, 2,000 troopers and 24 guns – about 8,000 in all – but Napoleon constantly added new units, enlarging the Guard into a corps and eventually into an army with its own support services. With many nationalities – Frenchmen, Belgians, Dutchmen, Poles, Mamelukes and others in its ranks – it embodied Napoleon's ambitions and was evidence of his continental empire. By 1805 its strength had risen to over 12,000 and in 1812 it numbered 56,000. Thereafter, its character became much diluted so that the 1814 figure of 112,482 men no longer represented only élite units.

Formed in 1804, the Imperial Guard was the corps d'élite *of the Grand Army. Its most prestigious element was the Old Guard, with the Grenadiers the senior infantry regiment. They were picked men. To be admitted to the Guard a soldier had to be at least 5 feet 6 ins tall, have served for a minimum of four years, and be a veteran of at least two campaigns. The Guard enjoyed substantial privileges: better pay, clothing, rations, and medical care than the rest of the army. Wearing full-dress uniforms on campaign, they provided part of Napoleon's personal escort, but he always considered them as his last reserve and hesitated before committing them to action. The picture here shows a corporal of Grenadiers, a rank equivalent to sergeant in a line regiment, guarding Napoleon's command group.*

The Guard was composed of three major and distinct elements. There were the regiments of the Old Guard, picked veterans with at least four years' service and two campaigns. The second element – the Middle Guard – was also highly selective and included some fine foreign troops. Finally, the Young Guard, which never quite attained the standards or the prestige of the senior regiments, enrolled the best recruits of each annual conscript class.

Napoleon separated the Imperial Guard from the rest of the army. It received better pay, quarters, rations, equipment and its own medical service, while individually each guardsman ranked one grade higher than his counterparts in the line. The emperor was particularly fond of its core elements, especially the grenadiers of the Old Guard, styled *les grognards* – the grumblers – and took a personal interest in their welfare. But he also hesitated to commit them to battle, preferring to hold them back as a last reserve: the sight of thousands of grenadiers in their tall bearskin caps – the Guard always fought in full dress – certainly impressed adversaries. In some major battles, Austerlitz and Borodino for example, the grenadiers were never committed and sometimes they were sent in too late. But when the Old Guard advanced then the climax of battle had arrived and it always was assumed that victory was assured. Still, the ultimate value of the Guard was debatable. It drained the line of many potential junior leaders and raised a morale problem. Held up as an example to the rest of the army, any failure in action would have grave consequences.

ARMING THE REVOLUTIONARY AND IMPERIAL ARMIES

The enlarged armies and the continued wars would hardly have been feasible without a major expansion in output of arms and ammunition, equipment and supplies. Weapons of course were the most critical requirement, though the retention of existing basic models helped to alleviate the problem. At the onset of the wars French arms production in 1792–3 fell to only 42,000 muskets, but rose considerably in the following years. The Committee of Public Safety established additional facilities, and for a short time they manufactured weapons in 'national workshops' in Paris and elsewhere. Mass production was achieved by employing as many workers as possible, and while machines were used in boring cannon and grinding metal parts, assembly and fitting had to be done by hand. As additional arms plants came on line from 1795 most French armies had a sufficient supply of muskets. Moreover, with almost all European muskets taking the same calibre ball, and with balls loose-fitting to allow for black powder fouling, captured weapons were widely utilized.

Under the Consulate and Empire small arms were again in short supply and Bonaparte accelerated production. Excluding the satellite states, the Empire ultimately manufactured a total of 3,926,257 small arms, but production never caught up with demand. By 1803 the French annual output was 125,000 weapons. Hanover furnished 40,000 muskets in 1804, smaller quantities were produced in Turin and in the Bavarian arsenal at Amberg. Many weapons were lost in combat; even a victory such as Austerlitz cost 12,000 muskets. Captured Austrian and Prussian arsenals helped to end shortages, but from 1808 on Spain became a constant drain on weapons. The 1812 campaign resulted in a near-critical situation, solved by issuing foreign weapons, captured or provided by German allies.

It was much the same with artillery. In 1793 Gaspard Monge, the distinguished mathematician and scientist in charge of artillery procurement, estimated France was 6,000 pieces of artillery short. To speed up production Monge invented a simplified casting method, built furnaces in converted churches and trained additional workmen. Copper for the bronze barrels was obtained by requisitioning church bells and through tacit trade with the enemy. Production expanded during the Consulate and the Empire and seventeen new foundries turned out an astonishing quantity, yet supply never caught up with demand even though much captured matériel was pressed into service. Although the Austrian ordnance was slightly outmatched by their French equivalents in throw weight, Napoleon was well impressed and used it widely. At

Wagram about one-third of his artillery was of Austrian origin, while light Prussian cannons were widely issued in Spain.

Finally, there was the propellant, black powder, required in ever-increasing quantities. The muskets were highly inaccurate and unreliable, and ammunition expenditure was enormous, perhaps half a million rounds in one battle. Yet, as one American observer notes, considering the number of rounds fired, 'the little execution done by muskets almost surpasses belief'. Lack of training combined with the thick smoke produced by black powder, careless loading and various malfunctions reduced the effects of infantry fire. Artillery, of course, required immense quantities of propellant, usually one-third the weight of the shot fired by the individual piece.

Britain increased weapons production even more sharply. In 1793, excluding weapons issued, there were only 60,000 muskets in reserve, and the government had to use the East India Company's extensive stocks. Some improvement followed in 1804 when the Board of Ordnance established its own assembly plants, and after 1808 arms production hit full stride. It had been difficult that year to find 200,000 pieces for the Peninsula, but by 1813 Britain equipped her own forces as well as providing over a million muskets for her various allies.

WAR RENEWED: THE THIRD COALITION

Peace was short-lived. While Napoleon consolidated his power at home, became Consul for Life in 1802 and on 2 December 1804 crowned himself Emperor of the French, his actions abroad affronted and threatened Europe. The uneasy peace with England broke down in the spring of 1803. The Royal Navy blockaded the French coast, while Napoleon went ahead with preparations to invade England. In Germany Napoleon occupied Hanover in the north and turned Bavaria and Württemberg into client states. He extended his control in Italy, with the Cisalpine Republic constituted as the Kingdom of Italy in 1805, ruled by a viceroy, his stepson Eugène de Beauharnais. Even Russia, ruled by the unstable Tsar

Alexander I who had favoured an accommodation with Napoleon, turned against him following the kidnapping and execution of the Duc d'Enghien in 1804. British diplomacy and gold contributed to forging the Third Coalition, but Napoleon's actions provided much of the impetus.

As always, Austria was supposed to provide the bulk of the land forces, but sentiment in Vienna was divided. The Emperor Francis I, a dignity he assumed following the demise of the Holy Roman Empire, and Archduke Charles, then trying to reform the Austrian army, were opposed to war. This changed when Napoleon accepted the Italian crown. Austria could not ignore this challenge and joined the Coalition on 9 August 1805, bolstered by promises of a huge British subsidy and the support of Russian armies. Sweden and Naples also signed on, while Prussia strongly hinted that it might join.

Napoleon's plan to lure the British fleet away from the Channel had failed and with it plans to invade England. In any case, Austrian mobilization along the Bavarian border and in Venetia constituted a threat. Although the failure of the naval plan was not yet evident, Napoleon decided to march against Austria before the Russians arrived. On 27 August 1805 the Grande Armée moved out from its cantonments to start upon two years of almost unbroken campaigning.

CHAPTER THREE

The Years of Victory 1805–7

Joining the Grande Armée in October, one Bavarian division commanded by General Deroy supported Ney's corps in the conquest of Tyrol. This picture shows the successful Bavarian action on 1 November 1805, when the Bodenmühl Pass was seized. In the foreground Bavarian Chevaux Légers and infantry attack Austrian artillery try to escape.

The Years of Victory

THE COALITION STRATEGY ENVISAGED an offensive that would sweep from the Baltic to the Adriatic. In the north a Russo-Swedish force was to attack west from Swedish Pomerania. To their left 40,000 Russians under the command of General Bennigsen were to support the Prussian army moving towards Hanover and Holland. An Austrian army, 89,000 strong, nominally commanded by Archduke Ferdinand, was to invade Bavaria and there wait for a Russian army of 55,000 men under the command of General Kutuzov, which would arrive in eastern Bavaria on 20 October, followed by General Buxhövden's army in Bohemia. Finally, multinational forces would conduct diversionary operations in southern Italy.

Austria regarded the reconquest of Lombardy as the most important objective. Therefore the largest Austrian army, some 100,000 men under Archduke Charles, was committed here. Archduke John, holding the Tyrol with 22,000 men, would serve as the link between Ferdinand and Charles, and great hopes were placed in the promised strategic diversions. In short, the allied, and in particular the Austrian, war plans lacked decisive concentration in a main theatre of operations. Separate armies in different theatres would conduct parallel campaigns.

Moreover, the king of Prussia preferred to accept Hanover as a bribe rather than risk war. Meanwhile there was confusion in the Austrian high command. General Mack, the ministerial favourite and in actual command on the Danube, pressed for an early entry into Bavaria, a move opposed by Charles who was prepared to advance in Italy but argued that the forces in Germany should await the arrival of the Russians. Initially, the Emperor Francis agreed with Charles, but then was persuaded to support Mack who confidently calculated that Napoleon could not appear in strength in Bavaria sooner than in sixty-nine days, while the Russians would arrive five days earlier. It was a fatal miscalculation.

NAPOLEON'S ADVERSARY: THE HABSBURG ARMY

The Austrian army, the largest land force continually engaged against the French Revolution and Napoleon, had remained a typical eighteenth-century, dynastic organization. Arch-conservative rulers and the multinational institutions of the Habsburg Empire inhibited radical changes. Yet, although it had been repeatedly defeated, this old-fashioned organization always managed to rise and fight again.

The army was the product of reforms following the Seven Years War when its fighting methods had been recast on the Prussian model. In 1792 its nominal strength was about 430,000 men, 57 regiments of line infantry, 17 *Grenzer* (peasant soldiers from the south-eastern frontier), 32 mounted regiments and 3 field artillery regiments. But with finances chronically in disarray the army was below establishment. The highest command agency was the *Hofkriegsrat* in Vienna, a military-civilian body making all matters exceedingly bureaucratic. The officer corps was aristocratic and international, with the highest commands reserved for members of the dynasty and the great noble families. In the lower grades family connections and birth mattered little and officers came from the lesser nobility, even the bourgeoisie. Promotion from the ranks was rare but possible; General Mack, considered an accomplished soldier, was one such exception.

Soldiers, conscripted and volunteer, came from the lower classes. Much resented, conscription was restricted to the hereditary lands – Austria, Bohemia and Moravia; in Hungary, the Tyrol, Galicia and Austrian Italy, being either privileged or thought unreliable, there was no conscription. When possible regiments recruited volunteers in the smaller German states, in Hungary and the Tyrol. Except for foreigners, service was for life and competent subalterns and sergeants produced highly disciplined soldiers.

Shortcomings had been highlighted in the earlier campaigns. The army lacked divisions and corps: its higher formations were temporary groupings and the absence of a permanent staff added to these problems. Commanders were competent, but their experience and outlook were out of date. They remained tied to their communications and overrated the value of linear tactics executed by well-drilled regiments. Austrian cavalry was considered among the best in the world. Mounts and horsemanship were excellent, but the cavalry had not been trained to fight in large formations. The same applied to the artillery: well equipped, well trained and numerous, but lacking structure and doctrine to deliver massed fire.

Although Austria had lost two wars against the French, the defeats had not been conclusive, and if there had been battles lost, there had also been victories. Vienna was not prepared to concede the need for systemic change, though the emperor was willing to try some modest reforms. In 1801 Archduke Charles, the victor of 1796, was appointed president of the *Hofkriegsrat*, but spent too much effort on administrative changes and too little on increasing combat effectiveness. He created a permanent staff organization, the Quartermaster General Staff, reduced conscript service to between ten and fourteen years, but failed to have Hungary accept conscription. Curiously, as war became more likely after 1803, his influence waned, while that of the war faction, civilian ministers with Mack as their chief military spokesman, rose. In 1805 the emperor reduced Charles's authority and appointed Mack chief of the Quartermaster General Staff, as well as de facto commander of the army in Germany. While Mack scrambled to make last-minute organizational changes, Charles found his army understrength and ill equipped, and decided not to risk an offensive in Italy. Then, and later, he lacked the driving will for victory and was reluctant to entrust the fate of the army, the guarantor of the dynasty, to battle.

The Austrians invaded Bavaria on 9 September; the Bavarian army, about 22,000 men, evaded to the north and eventually joined the French. Hasty mobilization and a rapid advance west beyond Munich to Ulm on the Iller River reduced Mack's effectives to around 50,000, hardly a number to impress Napoleon.

THE MANOEUVRE ON ULM

On 26 August Napoleon issued his orders. Altogether, he committed seven corps, the cavalry reserve and the Imperial Guard: a total of 200,000 men for the campaign in Germany. His basic plan was to assemble this force on the middle Rhine and the lower Main. From there he would push into Swabia, gather the forces of his south German allies and sweep behind the Austrian concentration which he assumed to be between the Iller and the Lech rivers, interposing his army between the Austrians and the approaching Russians, meaning to destroy each in turn.

The movement of such a large army was unprecedented. Marching along assigned roads the corps reached the line of departure, crossing the Rhine between 27 September and 2 October. Their concentration and direction were screened by Murat's six mounted divisions, which, together with Lannes's V Corps, managed to convince Mack that the French were attacking along the traditional invasion route through the Black Forest. After revealing to Ferdinand that he actually held command, Mack began to concentrate his forces around Ulm at the confluence of the Danube and Lech on 6 October. On the same day the French crossed the Danube further east, and brushing aside light opposition, isolated the Austrians from the Russians. As the encirclement closed Mack attempted to break out towards Bohemia but, lacking resolution, he failed to exploit a minor success on the north bank of the river on 11 October. During the next days one small detachment fled east and another ran south, but both were intercepted and annihilated. The last breakout came on 14 October: Archduke Ferdinand and 12 squadrons rode out of the doomed fortress, heading for Bohemia. From the next day on Mack was completely surrounded, with the Russians still some 180 kilometres to the east. On 20 October he surrendered the remains of his army, some 23,500 men. The manoeuvre on Ulm, 25 September to 20 October, was a classic example of a Napoleonic strike against the rear – the 1796 move on Piacenza repeated but on a much larger scale. In the space of four weeks a series

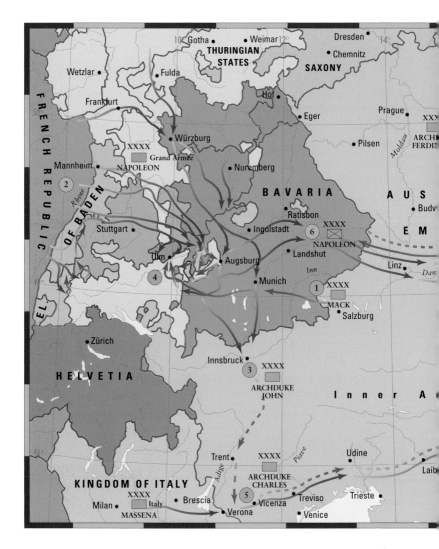

of well co-ordinated, tough marches had brought swift and complete victory. Soldiers observed that 'the Emperor makes war not with our arms but with our legs'. In the Ulm campaign Napoleon achieved his major objective – the annihilation of the enemy army – without fighting a major battle.

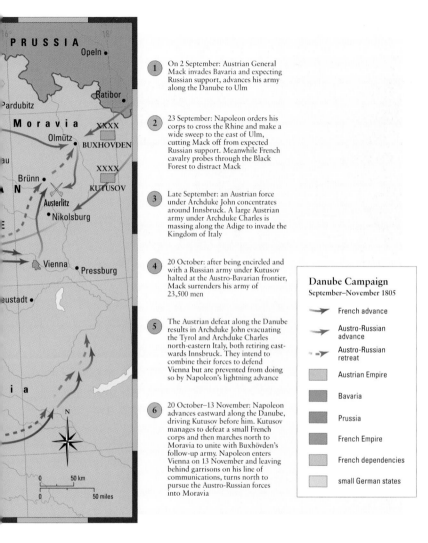

1 On 2 September: Austrian General Mack invades Bavaria and expecting Russian support, advances his army along the Danube to Ulm

2 23 September: Napoleon orders his corps to cross the Rhine and make a wide sweep to the east of Ulm, cutting Mack off from expected Russian support. Meanwhile French cavalry probes through the Black Forest to distract Mack

3 Late September: an Austrian force under Archduke John concentrates around Innsbruck. A large Austrian army under Archduke Charles is massing along the Adige to invade the Kingdom of Italy

4 20 October: after being encircled and with a Russian army under Kutusov halted at the Austro-Bavarian frontier, Mack surrenders his army of 23,500 men

5 The Austrian defeat along the Danube results in Archduke John evacuating the Tyrol and Archduke Charles north-eastern Italy, both retiring eastwards Innsbruck. They intend to combine their forces to defend Vienna but are prevented from doing so by Napoleon's lightning advance

6 20 October–13 November: Napoleon advances eastward along the Danube, driving Kutusov before him. Kutusov manages to defeat a small French corps and then marches north to Moravia to unite with Buxhövden's follow-up army. Napoleon enters Vienna on 13 November and leaving behind garrisons on his line of communications, turns north to pursue the Austro-Russian forces into Moravia

Danube Campaign
September–November 1805

→ French advance

→ Austro-Russian advance

- -→ Austro-Russian retreat

Austrian Empire

Bavaria

Prussia

French Empire

French dependencies

small German states

THE WAR IN ITALY

In Italy Massena was directed to stand on the defensive, while the archduke had decided to do the same. Charles greatly over-estimated Massena's forces and was convinced that the expected disaster in Germany made it his primary duty to preserve what might well be the

Habsburgs' last field army. Both sides agreed to an armistice, subject to six days notice, until 11 October. Informed that the Grande Armée had arrived on its Rhine–Main departure line, Massena decided to attack, and on 18 October managed to cross the Adige river. But Charles had already retired some kilometres east to Caldiero where he hoped to inflict enough damage on Massena to deter him from pursuing his retreat north. For three days, 29 to 31 October, the French attacked the entrenched and numerically slightly superior Austrians. On the third day, after both sides had suffered heavy casualties, Charles retired, pursued by Massena into the Julian Alps.

THE MARCH ON VIENNA

The 'unfortunate General Mack' disposed of, Napoleon turned against Kutuzov who had assembled some 27,000 troops, only half the number promised, on the River Inn where some 16,000 Austrians joined him. Despite pleas by Emperor Francis to defend Vienna, Kutuzov, intent on joining Buxhövden in Moravia, retired east along the right side of the Danube, crossing to the left bank at Mautern on 9 November where two days later he mauled Marshal Mortier's hastily formed VIII Corps, just 7,500 strong. Napoleon shifted Bernadotte's corps across to support Mortier, while the bulk of the French Army, Murat's cavalry leading, moved on Vienna.

The Austrians made no attempt to defend their capital or deny stores to the conquerors. Much attention was given to evacuating the archives, but tens of thousands of muskets, hundreds of cannons, ammunition, and depots were left behind. On 12 November elements of Lannes's corps and Murat's cavalry entered Vienna, and the next morning the two marshals captured the principal bridge over the Danube, without firing a shot, by convincing the senior officer present that an armistice had come into force. The failure to deny the bridge demonstrated the lack of will and intellect prevailing in the Austrian higher command in 1805.

Kutuzov, however, recognized the danger posed by the French main force across the Danube and accelerated his movement north towards

Brünn, posting Prince Bagration with 8,000 men as a rearguard at Schöngrabern. On 15 November Bagration in turn bluffed Murat into halting operations, and, when attacked the following day, his tenacious resistance bought time for Kutuzov to join Buxhövden three days later near Olmütz. The combined armies now numbered 71,000, and, when joined by 15,000 Austrians, the Allies disposed of 86,000 combatants. At this point Tsar Alexander, who fancied himself a general, assumed personal command.

THE RUSSIAN ARMY AND THE ROAD TO AUSTERLITZ
The stand at Schöngrabern highlighted one of the Russian army's major assets – the stolid bravery of its conscripted serf soldiers. Fearless in attack, the Russians were perhaps even better on the defence. Conscripted for life, soldiers were allowed to marry, their children conscripted, drilled and indoctrinated from an early age. Discipline was brutal and religion a powerful, motivating force, inspiring soldiers as they fought the enemy – infidel, Moslem, heretic or atheist.

The officer corps had serious shortcomings. Generally it was drawn from the Russian upper classes, nobles and gentry, but contained some foreign elements. The great majority of regimental officers came from the gentry and started their careers as non-commissioned officers. Poorly educated, often hardly literate, they normally spent their lives as obscure infantry or artillery officers. Hardy and loyal, they were also negligent and incapable of making decisions on their own. The nobility entered the army through a number of cadet schools and took up commissions in the Guards or in élite mounted regiments. As a group they were cultured though not educated, and lacked competence for administrative or staff duties. None the less, they often managed to be assigned to higher headquarters. Napoleon is reported to have said that a French private took more interest in the planning and conduct of a battle than senior Russian officers. Plainly this was an unjust slur on men like Suvorov or Kutuzov, but it fitted the many young aristocrats who crowded the tsar's entourage. Under these circumstances administrative and staff work often fell to officers of foreign extraction who were much resented, or even to foreign nationals. Austrian staff officers were assigned to the Russian operational armies, frequently as chiefs of staff to army commanders. At Austerlitz General Weyrother, an Austrian, served as chief of staff to Kutuzov.

Russia found it difficult to mobilize its manpower potential and to project force beyond its borders. The armies sent to help the Austrians and British were poorly equipped and lacked logistic support. The army, organized into twelve territorial districts, or Inspections – nine in Europe, three in Asia – divided into three major elements: the Guard, the Line and the Cossacks. No higher tactical formations existed. Units were assigned by regiment, squadron or battery to field commanders. The Russians were badly outmatched by the Grande Armée in battle engaging corps-size formations and requiring generalship, command, control, co-ordination, intelligence and tactical flexibility.

THE BATTLE OF AUSTERLITZ

By the end of November Napoleon, with his main force at Brünn, 97 kilometres north of Vienna, faced serious problems. After detaching troops to cover the flanks and rear of his deep penetration along the Danube and into Moravia, his combat strength was down to 70,000 men, facing a substantially stronger opponent who seemed about to move out of reach. To the south, only fourteen marching days away, Archduke Charles was assembling an army of 85,000, and there were signs that Prussia might join the Coalition. Napoleon needed one great victory that would shatter the Coalition and to this end was determined to lure the enemy into launching an attack on ground suitable for a protracted defence where a sudden counterstroke would destroy him.

THE BATTLE OF AUSTERLITZ, 2 DECEMBER 1805 (I)

Raig

Vienna

1 1 December: to induce the enemy (71,000 Russians and 15,000 Austrians) to attack on ground of his choosing, Napoleon exposes his army with its right flank weak and even evacuates the Pratzen Heights

2 Reinforcements are already on the way, especially Davout's corps marching from Vienna and expected to arrive at 6 am the next day

3 On 2 December the Russians attack across the Pratzen Heights, then swerve obliquely north of Satschan Pond to attack Davout.

4 Meanwhile, on the left flank, Lannes' and Murat's cavalry engage a Russian force under Bagration and fight it to a standstill

5 The Russian movement across the Pratzen Heights has disordered their battle line and at 9.30 am, with Davout holding, Napoleon orders Soult to retake the heights and then fall on the rear of the Russians

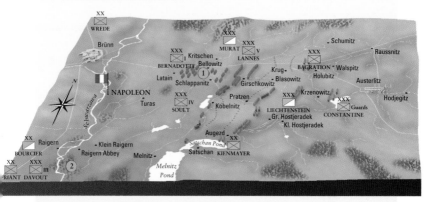

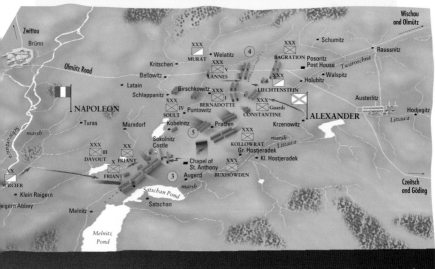

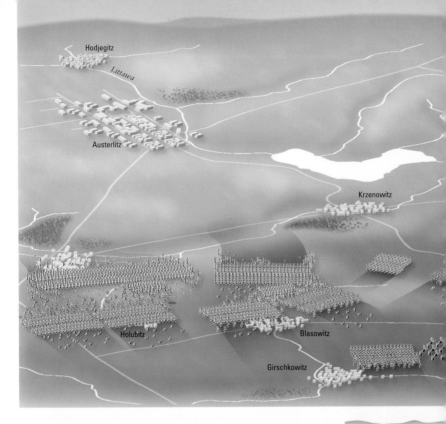

6 Attempts by the Russian Guard to counter-attack Soult fail. At about 11 am Soult begins to move against the Russian rear

7 Almost totally enveloped, with Davout moving to the attack at 1 pm, the Russians rout east across the marshes and frozen ponds. Meanwhile Lannes advances, while Bernadotte drives towards Austerlitz. When dusk falls fighting ends with the Allied army no longer combat capable

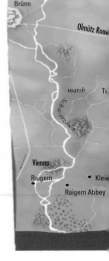

THE BATTLE OF AUSTERLITZ, 2 DECEMBER 1805 (II)

Perhaps Napoleon's most decisive battle, the battle of Austerlitz practically destroyed the Russo-Austrian army, forcing Austria to accept a costly peace, while compelling the Russians to withdraw east.

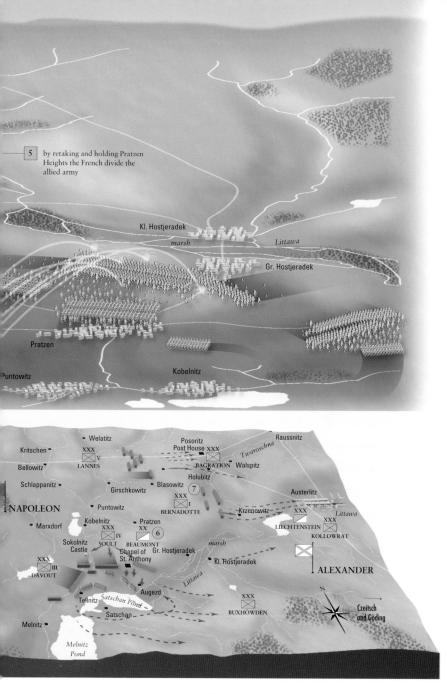

5 by retaking and holding Pratzen Heights the French divide the allied army

Kl. Hostjeradek

marsh   *Littawa*

Gr. Hostjeradek

Pratzen

Puntowitz   Kobelnitz

Welatitz

Kritschen

XXX V
LANNES

Bellowitz

Posoritz
Post House   XXX

Raussnitz

Twaroschna

BAGRATION   Walspitz

Schlappanitz

Girschkowitz   Blasowitz

Holubitz

7

Austerlitz

NAPOLEON

Puntowitz

XXX I
BERNADOTTE

Krzenowitz

XXX
LIECHTENSTEIN

Littawa

XXX
KOLLOWRAT

Kobelnitz

Marxdorf

XXX IV
SOULT

Pratzen

XX   6
BEAUMONT

Sokolnitz
Castle

Chapel of
St. Anthony

Gr. Hostjeradek

marsh

Kl. Hostjeradek

XXX
ALEXANDER

XXX III
DAVOUT

Littawa

Augezd

Telnitz   Satschan Pond

XXX
BUXHÖWDEN

N

Czeitsch
and Göding

Satschan

Melnitz

*Melnitz
Pond*

He had already selected his battlefield, a naturally strong position about 20 kilometres east of Brünn, parallel with the Vienna–Brünn road. Here the terrain was wooded, broken by low valleys, with scattered marshes and ponds and the Goldbach brook, behind which his right wing could hold off the enemy, while his concealed *masse de rupture* waited to deliver the counterstroke in the centre. To entice the enemy to attack he feigned weakness, requesting an armistice on 27 November, retreating from his forward positions in apparent disorder, abandoning the village of Austerlitz and the Pratzen Heights. Overruling Kutuzov, Tsar Alexander decided to accept battle and adopted a plan to threaten Napoleon's communications with Vienna. Moving west from Olmütz the allied main force would, after passing Austerlitz, angle south-west to crush the French right. After that it would pivot to roll up – drive in on itself – the remainder of Napoleon's army.

Once Napoleon became aware that the enemy had swallowed his bait he ordered the outlying corps of Bernadotte and Davout to join him by forced marches. On 1 December he had 66,000 men and 139 guns. Lannes's corps, with Murat's cavalry, anchored his left flank just above the Olmütz–Brünn highway. Soult's corps thinly covered the centre and the right flank of the French line. The counterstroke force was concealed north-west of the Pratzen plateau. The night before the battle, following an unusual meeting with his marshals, Napoleon shifted Soult's corps north-west, leaving the defence on the extreme right flank to Davout, who was expected to arrive early in the morning.

Meanwhile at allied headquarters it was believed that Napoleon planned to withdraw. Weyrother, a student of Frederick the Great, explained his oblique multi-column attack to the Russian and Austrian generals, though with excellent Austrian survey maps available he should have realized that the columns might bog down in the difficult terrain. Kutuzov, who opposed the plan, slept through most of the proceedings.

In the dense mist of dawn, on 2 December, the Allies attacked. In essence there were three separate and simultaneous engagements. The most critical was in the south where 40,000 allied infantry, mainly

Russian, pounded obliquely forward from the Pratzen, their advance hampered in terrain where large numbers could not deploy effectively. Arriving at the last moment, Davout managed to contain them west of the Goldbach. Fighting was heavy, with positions changing hands several times.

Meanwhile, across from the Pratzen plateau, Napoleon observed Buxhövden's columns moving south off the high ground, weakening the Russian centre. This was the moment the emperor had been waiting for. At about 9.30 a.m., with the sun – the sun of Austerlitz – breaking through the clouds, he ordered Soult to retake the Pratzen with two divisions. By 11 the plateau was in French hands. Shortly after noon a countercharge by the Russian Imperial Guard regained some ground, but was thrown back when Napoleon committed his Guard cavalry and elements of Bernadotte's corps. The allied centre disintegrated, while Soult continued southward from the Pratzen against the flank and rear of the now isolated Russo-Austrian mass floundering in the valley of the Goldbach. As they routed across the swamps and partially frozen ponds, the secondary allied attack in the north also had failed. Although night and exhaustion prevented pursuit, it was a crushing defeat. The Allies lost nearly a third of their number: 11,000 Russians and 4,000 Austrians killed, and another 12,000 prisoners, along with 180 guns and about 50 flags, compared to a total of 9,000 French casualties. The allied army had ceased to exist as a fighting force.

Austerlitz was Napoleon's perfect battle – not an 'ordinary' victory, but the annihilation of a powerful opponent. Its outcome changed everything. Prussia, prepared to intervene, hastily accepted Napoleon's offer of Hanover in return for its benevolent neutrality. The Russians withdrew into Poland, while on 6 December Austria agreed to a truce, followed on the 26th by the Treaty of Pressburg. It ceded Venetia, Dalmatia and Istria to Napoleon's Kingdom of Italy and accorded royal status to Napoleon's German allies, the rulers of Württemberg, Baden and Bavaria, the last receiving Vorarlberg and the Tyrol, preparing the way for the Confederation of the Rhine the following year.

In the meantime the minor allied operations had also failed. The British and Swedes had achieved little in Hanover, while the British-supported Neapolitans had been chased from the mainland to Sicily. On 27 December 1805 Napoleon's brother Joseph was proclaimed King of Naples; in May 1806 the Batavian Republic became the Kingdom of Holland under Napoleon's older brother Louis. Perhaps the only bright spot for England was the encounter at Maida in Calabria on 6 July 1806, where a small British expedition fighting in line defeated a stronger French force attacking in column. And perhaps a portent of the future, throughout Calabria aroused peasants continued their bitter small war against the French.

THE PRUSSIAN ARMY AND THE JENA CAMPAIGN

Prussia had received Hanover as a bribe for its neutrality, but early in 1806 Napoleon demanded that Prussia cede him Neuchâtel in Switzerland, as well as some lands in Germany. Finally, Prussia learned that Napoleon was willing to return Hanover to Britain in return for peace. This was more than King Frederick William III, already pressured by a war party at court and by an officer corps remembering the days of the Great Frederick, could accept. In July he concluded a secret alliance with Alexander and began to prepare for war. But he was alone. The Russians were far away, forming two field armies around Brest-Litovsk, while the unwilling Hanoverian conscripts and the small contingents from Brunswick (Braunschweig) and Hesse-Kassel counted for little. To gain more manpower, on 12 September Frederick William ordered his troops into Saxony to compel this state to join him. As yet there was no declaration of war. Deployed in a 150-kilometre-wide arc along Saxony's south-western frontier, the Prussians grossly overestimated their power. On 26 September they issued an ultimatum demanding that Napoleon withdraw his troops from Germany. Thus began the war of the Fourth Coalition, with Sweden and Britain eventually joining Prussia and Russia.

The disaster that followed could have been foreseen. Prussia was isolated – invoking the glorious past could not conceal the fact that the army had become a museum piece. Despite the experiences of the war against France, combat doctrine and methods remained Frederician. The infantry stressed the three-rank linear formation, controlled volleys and steady advances. Cavalry could charge, but could not do so in large formations. The field artillery was obsolescent, too heavy for tactical mobility, but Prussia, maintaining an army whose upkeep exceeded its resources, could afford neither to replace its artillery nor the outworn Model 1754 muskets.

It would have been possible to reorganize the highest command agencies where civilian ministers and generals squabbled, or to incorporate some of the lessons of the Revolutionary and Napoleonic Wars into the tactical system. Efforts were made. In 1795 a new command agency, the *Oberkriegskollegium*, was created to streamline administration, but, representing the various agencies, it naturally did nothing. As for tactics, especially open order and skirmishing, a few independent light battalions were established, but not integrated into the tactical scheme. Finally, when the army was already marching, all-arms divisional formations were hastily introduced, but only added further to the confusion.

Resistance to change could be found in the character of the king, a military enthusiast overly concerned with minutiae, and the obstinacy of the proud and almost entirely noble overaged officer corps. In 1806, of the 142 generals in the Prussian Army, four were over the age of eighty, including the king's senior military adviser, Fieldmarshal von Möllendorf, an 82-year-old veteran of Leuthen. Of the remainder

OVERLEAF: THE COLLAPSE OF PRUSSIA, 1806

Having refrained from supporting Austria and Russia in 1805, Prussia challenged Napoleon the next year. But Prussian strategy was indecisive and divided her army into two major sections. Moving out from cantonments in southern Germany, the Grande Armée crushed the Prussians on 14 October at Jena and Auerstädt. Immediate and relentless cavalry pursuit destroyed the remaining field forces as the Prussian state collapsed. By November, there only remained a small Prussian corps in East Prussia and some isolated fortress garrisons in Silesia and East Prussia.

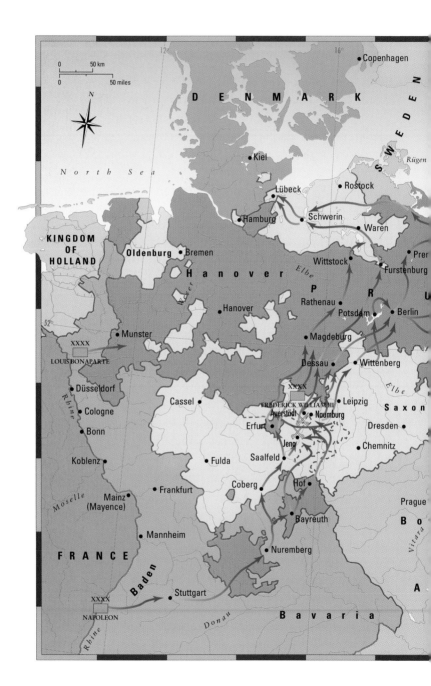

The Prussian Collapse
1806

→ French advance

- -➤ Prussian retreat

⌒ initial Prussian
deployment

⚔ site of battle

thirteen were over 70, and sixty were over the age of 60, while fully a quarter of the regimental and battalion commanders were in the same age group – survivors from the age of limited war. The principal Prussian field commander was the 71-year-old Duke of Brunswick who had been defeated at Valmy.

The Prussian Army was based on conscription. Nominally, all subjects were liable to serve but there were numerous exemptions. Foreigners continued to make up well over one half of the army's strength, which, all included, stood at about 245,000 in 1806, though after deducting garrison and depot troops, as well as General Lestocq's division left behind in East Prussia, field strength was only about 140,000 men. Though poorly led, the men would give a surprisingly good account of themselves, in many ways better than that of their superior officers.

THE JENA–AUERSTÄDT CAMPAIGN

Following the 1805 campaign, the Grande Armée had not returned to France but remained quartered in southern Germany and along the Rhine. Only the Imperial Guard had accompanied Napoleon to Paris. When war seemed unavoidable 3,700 men of the Guard infantry were hurriedly transported by wagon relays to the Rhine, arriving on 28 September. Napoleon planned to take the offensive, in simplest terms repeating the manoeuvre on Ulm, getting between the Prussians and their capital and defeating them before the Russians could intervene. Only leaving behind his Dutch forces in Holland and a corps forming under Mortier along the Rhine, he assembled his corps between Bamberg and Würzburg before moving north-east into Saxony and towards Berlin. The army deployed in broad front 'battalion square', three massive columns of two corps each, marching on parallel roads within supporting distance of each other and able to swing to the left or the right. On 8 October the army, covered by a light cavalry screen, disappeared into the Thuringian Forest.

The Prussians had formed two armies, the main under Brunswick, the second under Prince Hohenlohe-Ingelfingen. They had decided to concentrate in the Weimar–Jena area but were still on the move when on 10 October the vanguard of Lannes's V Corps hit the advance guard of Hohenlohe's army at Saalfeld. Losing fewer than 200 casualties, Lannes wiped out nearly half the Prussian force, capturing thirty-three guns and 1,800 prisoners. This local defeat demoralized Brunswick, who ordered both Prussian armies to fall back to the Elbe and Berlin. But this order came too late. By 12 October the battalion square had moved around the left flank of the withdrawing Prussians. The next day Napoleon wheeled the bulk of his forces westward against what he presumed to be the main Prussian force at Jena, sending Davout some 18 kilometres north to strike the enemy's rear. Davout was to be followed by Bernadotte who, in hasty instructions, was given discretion either to join Davout or to continue on to a central position at Dornburg. On 14 October two battles with fronts reversed were fought. At Jena Napoleon faced only Hohenlohe's army, while to the north, at Auerstädt, Davout's single corps encountered the bulk of the Prussian Army commanded by Brunswick. Throughout that desperate day Bernadotte, disregarding Napoleon's axiom to 'always march to the sound of the guns', did nothing.

Napoleon, assuming that he faced the main Prussian Army, ordered up Soult, Augerau and Ney to reinforce Lannes's leading corps, retaining the Guard in reserve. When the battle opened around 6.30 a.m. Napoleon had 55,000 men available, to be joined by another 40,000 by noon. The Prussians had only 38,000, with another 15,000 men 12 kilometres distant at Weimar, but these only managed to arrive in the afternoon to participate in Hohenlohe's defeat. Given the odds, the outcome of the battle was never really in doubt. The Prussians fought bravely; their infantry counter-attacking in near-parade order, they held until noon. Then they conducted a fighting retreat, but in the early afternoon retreat turned into a rout with Murat's cavalry pursuing the fugitives. When losses were counted those of the French amounted to about 5,000; the Prussians lost 25,000 men, 200 guns, and 30 flags.

While Napoleon fought what he believed was the main Prussian body, Davout's III Corps – 26,000 men, 44 guns – collided with the bulk of the enemy's army – 64,000 men, 230 guns – led by Brunswick and accompanied by the king, just north of Auerstädt. Forming squares whenever Prussian cavalry charged and somewhat shielded by thick fog from heavy artillery fire, Davout gradually brought his three divisions into action. By mid morning the pressure against the French centre began to mount, but at this point Brunswick was mortally wounded and the king failed to take effective command. Regaining the initiative, Davout pushed his flanking divisions forward, pivoting against the Prussian flanks, a textbook double envelopment. Although the Prussian reserve had not yet been engaged, the army began to break up and, not realizing that the battle there was lost, fled towards Jena, meeting the thousands of fugitives streaming north. All cohesion vanished as Prussia's field army virtually ceased to exist.

A romantic picture of Napoleon and his suite passing his Old Guard Grenadiers, who are presenting arms, during the battle of Jena, 14 October 1806. Napoleon granted considerable leeway to his men and merely looks astonished as a grognard *in the second rank lifts his bearskin cap to shout a greeting.*

This was Davout's most brilliant battle, fought against odds greater even than at Austerlitz. The price was high. He lost almost one-quarter of his effectives, but inflicted 12,000 casualties and took 3,000 prisoners and 115 guns. Napoleon at first refused to believe what had happened, and then was slow to recognize the marshal's achievement. Curiously, Bernadotte was reprimanded only for his failure to show up at either battle. The two battles, with their inadequate reconnaissance, occasional lack of co-operation or even competence among subordinates, were redeemed by the fighting performance of the troops, the whole driven by an enormous energy and purpose at the very top so characteristic of Napoleonic warfare. This time, unlike Austerlitz, victory was followed by an unrelenting pursuit during which Murat's cavalry covered 600 kilometres in twenty-three days, while on 26 October Davout's corps was given the honour of being the first to enter Berlin.

Jena and Auerstädt were no disgrace to the Prussians, who had been outnumbered almost two to one in the first, and fought bravely in the second battle. The real disgrace was the collapse of the army and state in the days following the defeat. Attempts to rally troops failed as panicky commanders surrendered without a fight, and fortresses capitulated when summoned. A few areas on the Baltic shore and in Silesia held out, and General Blücher's force made a fighting retreat to Lübeck where it was forced to surrender on 7 November. Beyond the Oder River some troops escaped the contagion, but the state of Frederick II had vanished. And yet the virtual destruction of the Prussian forces – the greatest triumph of Napoleon's strategy of annihilation – did not end the war. From Königsberg in East Prussia Frederick William rejected Napoleon's terms, his resolve stiffened by his strong-willed queen and the promise of Russian support.

THE WINTER CAMPAIGN IN EAST PRUSSIA AND POLAND

Britain had limited her war effort to peripheral operations in the Mediterranean and Latin America, while subsidizing the other members of the Coalition. To undermine her ability to continue as paymaster Napoleon resolved on economic warfare. From Berlin, in November 1806, he decreed the Continental System, declaring a blockade of the British Isles and closing all French-controlled ports to British trade. If largely ineffective, attempts to enforce and expand the system drove Napoleon into further and ever more costly wars. At the same time he could not ignore the massing Russian forces near Grodno.

Russian army organization had improved. There now existed 18 large all-arms divisions, each with 6 foot regiments, 20 squadrons of horse and 82 guns. Russia mobilized two armies: one under General Count Bennigsen, a soldier of Hanoverian extraction, a competent cavalry leader but lacking experience fighting Napoleon; the second commanded by Buxhövden. Together these armies, comprising 90,000 men and 452 guns, compelled Napoleon into eight more months of fighting.

In November Bennigsen moved into central Poland, but on the approach of Davout, followed by Lannes, Soult and Murat, he retired across the Vistula to concentrate around Pultusk from where he threatened Napoleon's communications. In late December Napoleon tried to destroy Bennigsen through another *manoeuvre sur les derrières*, but weather and road conditions prevented execution of the plan and Bennigsen was able to retire north. Napoleon realized that he was nearing the end of his operational range and that troop morale was low. In Poland it was impossible to live off the land. There were substantial magazines in Prussia, but poor roads and difficult weather hampered movement of supplies. But with Bennigsen pushed north, Napoleon was able to disperse his army into winter quarters spread across a vast area north of Warsaw.

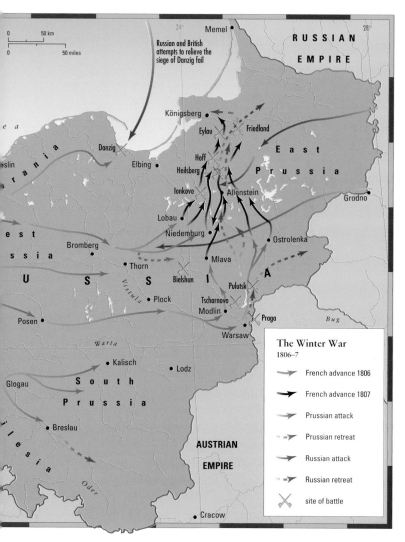

The Winter War
1806–7

→ French advance 1806
→ French advance 1807
→ Prussian attack
-→ Prussian retreat
→ Russian attack
-→ Russian retreat
✕ site of battle

NAPOLEON'S CAMPAIGN IN POLAND AND EAST PRUSSIA 1807

This campaign, including the bloody battles of Eylau and Friedland, was fought primarily around Königsberg, a port in Prussian hands and a major supply base for the Russian armies in Poland. With communications in Poland extremely poor, Napoleon needed Danzig, also still held by Prussia, as a supply port, but it fell only on 27 May, two weeks before his decisive victory at Friedland.

Holding court there, he hinted at future Polish independence and enlisted Polish troops. Two Polish and two Italian divisions, joined by a Baden contingent, evidence that the Grande Armée was becoming an international body, were formed as a provisional corps under Marshal Lefebvre to invest Prussian-held Danzig, though at this time no close siege was possible. Napoleon needed the port to ease his supply problem. Also, still thinking of possibilities in the Near East, Napoleon managed to incite the sultan into war against Russia, diverting some 20,000 men.

Fighting flared up again at the end of January 1807 when Bennigsen pushed against Ney and Bernadotte on the left sector of the French line. Napoleon perceived this as another opportunity to trap Bennigsen by driving between him and Königsberg, but his orders fell into Russian hands and Bennigsen retired north to Eylau, 33 kilometres south of Königsberg. Here, with Lestocq's Prussians in supporting range, and aware that the French corps were still separated, he decided to fight. Murat and Soult arrived before Eylau during the late afternoon of 7 February, followed by Augereau and finally Napoleon and the Guard. The French occupied the town, the Russians camped on the frozen fields. The next morning, 8 February, Napoleon found almost 70,000 Russians, their artillery outnumbering his by more than two to one, deployed against his 45,000 soldiers, and only then sent for Davout and Ney. He intended a double envelopment – Ney attacking on the left and Davout on the right, while Soult and Augereau engaged frontally. Soult was repulsed, while Augereau, losing bearings in a sudden blizzard, marched headlong into the fire of seventy guns. His corps disintegrated, opening a gap in the French line into which Bennigsen launched a counter-attack that penetrated into Eylau.

Bennigsen might have won the battle, but missed his moment. In one of history's great cavalry charges, Murat's 10,700 crashed through the Russians. At a cost of about 1,500 casualties the charge had unbalanced the Russian centre and allowed Davout's advance elements to attack the Russian left flank. By late afternoon the Russians began to waver, but were saved by Lestocq's arrival. They advanced on Davout's open right flank, but at 7 p.m. Ney, who had received his orders late, arrived to

The siege of Danzig, 18 March – 27 May 1807. This well-defended major port was invested and then besieged by X Corps, primarily Confederation of the Rhine troops, under Marshal Lefebvre.

strike at the Russian left. Bennigsen broke off combat and retired in good order. Losses on both sides were heavy. French casualties numbered between 20,000 and 25,000, while the Russians lost 11,000 and left 2,500 prisoners behind. There could be no pursuit and Napoleon could only claim victory because he was left in possession of the field. In reality, at best it was a draw. Riding over the field the next morning Ney exclaimed: 'What a massacre! And without result.'

After Eylau Napoleon was forced to return to winter quarters to rest, re-equip, and rebuild his depleted forces. French conscripts and a growing number of foreign troops augmented his armies, dispersed throughout Europe, to almost 600,000. An army of observation in Germany backed up the Grande Armée in Poland, a total of nearly 400,000 men, though only 100,000 would participate in the summer offensive. To support this the emperor brought Massena from Italy to Poland and ordered Lefebvre, who had been diverted south to guard communications, to renew and speed up the capture of Danzig.

THE BATTLE OF FRIEDLAND, 13–14 JUNE 1807

Attempting to destroy Lannes's corps, Bennigsen pushed several corps across the River Alle on the evening and night of 13 June. But Lannes held, was reinforced, and when Napoleon and additional forces arrived in the afternoon, the Russians were caught with their backs to a river and suffered very heavy casualties.

2 During the morning Lannes manages to delay the Russian advance. Bennigsen contents himself to deploy his troops around Friedland

1 After skirmishing the previous evening, on 14 June 1807, Bennigsen crosses the river Alle with 46,000 men and moves against Lannes' 17,000 French troops

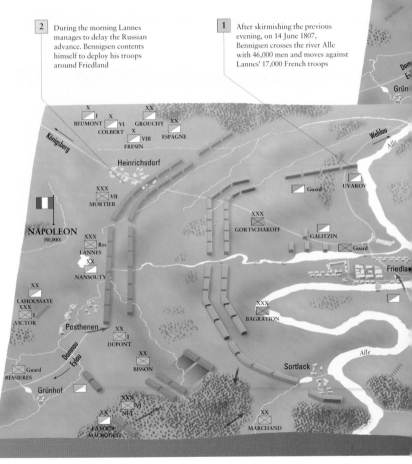

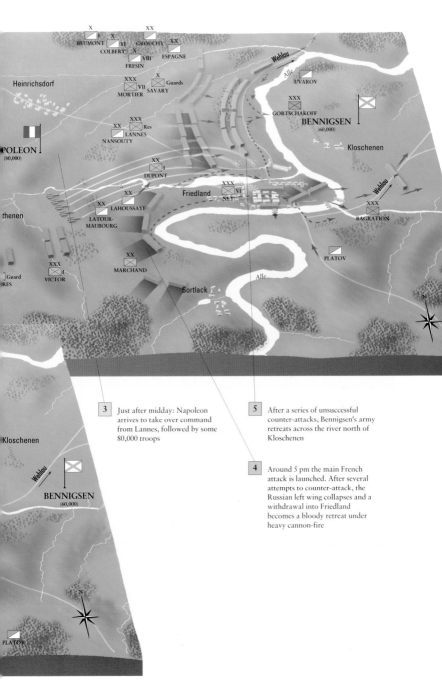

X
BEUMONT
I

X
COLBERT
VI

XX
GROUCHY

XX
ESPAGNE

X
FRESIN
VIII

Weblau

Alle

XXX
UVAROV

XXX
MORTIER
VII

X
SAVARY
Guards

Heinrichsdorf

XXX
GORTSCHAKOFF

BENNIGSEN
(60,000)

XXX
BENNIGSEN

Kloschenen

XXX
Res

XX
LANNES

NANSOUTY

POLEON
(80,000)

XX
DUPONT

Friedland

XXX
NEY
VI

Weblau

XXX
BAGRATION

thenen

XX
LAHOUSSAYE

XX
LATOUR-
MAUBOURG

XXX
I

VICTOR

XX
MARCHAND

Guard
RES

PLATOV

Sortlack

Alle

N

Kloschenen

Weblau

BENNIGSEN
(60,000)

N

PLATOV

3 Just after midday: Napoleon arrives to take over command from Lannes, followed by some 80,000 troops

5 After a series of unsuccessful counter-attacks, Bennigsen's army retreats across the river north of Kloschenen

4 Around 5 pm the main French attack is launched. After several attempts to counter-attack, the Russian left wing collapses and a withdrawal into Friedland becomes a bloody retreat under heavy cannon-fire

After an old-fashioned, three-month siege the fortress surrendered on 27 May, easing Napoleon's supply problem and releasing 20,000 men to fight against Bennigsen, who had rebuilt his forces to about 90,000 regulars and some 8,000 Cossacks.

Again, Napoleon intended to destroy Bennigsen by cutting him off from his base at Königsberg. After repelling a Russian offensive and driving Bennigsen out of his fortified camp at Heilsberg on 10 June, he divided his forces. He sent Murat and Soult, with Davout in support, to capture Königsberg, while Lannes probed along the west side of the Alle river. On 13 June Bennigsen discovered Lannes and ordered several divisions across the river to destroy what he thought was an isolated division. Advance elements clashed during the evening near Friedland, a small town 43 kilometres south of Königsberg, and during the night the Russians built up to 60,000 men. Fighting from well-chosen positions Lannes held until the first reinforcements from Mortier's corps appeared on the morning of 14 June. Soon, some 35,000 French were in action. Napoleon arrived shortly after noon with almost 50,000 men behind him. He realized immediately that the Russians were in an impossible position – outnumbered, on the wrong side of an unfordable river and connected to the rear by just three pontoon bridges.

By four in the afternoon Napoleon had 80,000 men available and an hour later he gave orders to attack. The first assault went in on the right along the Alle, followed by a frontal attack in the centre pressing the Russians into the curvature of the river. General Sénarmont, I Corps' chief of artillery, advanced a 30-gun battery by stages into canister range to open up on the packed Russians. Fighting in Friedland and environs lasted into the night. Russian losses were at least 30,000, but French casualties were not light: 10,000 in all, 1,400 killed.

Friedland was no easy victory, but it did much to revive the morale of the army shaken by Eylau and the miseries of winter in Poland. It introduced a new style of battle tactics, with massed artillery paving the way for the infantry assault. Also, Friedland was the first battle in which a major part of his army had not been French, illustrating the emperor's increasing manpower problems. But for the moment the Grande Armée could rest and look with pride on its exploits since leaving the encampments along the Channel two long years before.

The battle also ended the Third Coalition. On 7 July, at Tilsit, the two emperors met on a raft afloat the River Niemen to arrange the future of Europe. Losing about one third of her territory, paying a heavy indemnity, with her army reduced to 42,000 and French garrisons in her cities, Prussia effectively became a French satellite. The tsar, aligned with the French, agreed to join the Continental System – Napoleon's attempt at economic warfare which banned British trade with French-controlled areas. At Tilsit Napoleon stood at the zenith of his power.

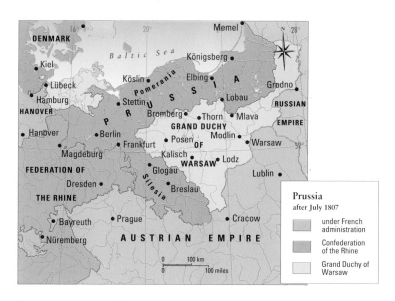

PRUSSIA AFTER THE TREATY OF TILSIT

The Treaty of Tilsit in July 1807 resulted in Prussia losing almost one-third of her territory; she gave up all land taken in the partitions of Poland, and all her territory between the Elbe and the Rhine. Her army was reduced to 42,000 men.

CHAPTER FOUR

The Grande Armée, Spain and the Habsburg Recovery 1807–9

Within the limitations of available technology, Napoleon tried to control his battles closely. Here he is shown at the critical point of the battle, shortly after noon on the second day of Wagram, 6 July 1809, observing Davout's envelopment of the extreme left of the Austrian position at Markgrafneusiedl.

The Grande Armée, Spain
and the Habsburg Recovery

FOLLOWING TILSIT, NAPOLEON DOMINATED Europe from the Pyrenees to the Russian border. Only Britain remained defiant, though even here war weariness and financial problems might have induced the government to make a settlement provided the French emperor had been willing to restore some degree of balance of power in Europe. But Napoleon's craving for domination left no room for compromise. He pursued his economic warfare against British trade, and when Portugal flouted his demands he decided to occupy the country, becoming embroiled on the Iberian Peninsula where even a small British force could be effective. French setbacks here encouraged Austria to mount another challenge.

THE GRANDE ARMÉE: FOREIGN AND ALLIED TROOPS

Napoleon paid little attention to losses and boasted that he could replace 30,000 men a month. Even so, he could not absorb losses on the scale of Eylau or Friedland. To fill his ranks he was compelled to fall back on men previously deferred and from 1806 he also called annual classes in advance. In addition, conscription was extended to annexed territories. By 1803 these included Belgium, the left bank of the Rhine, Savoy, Nice and Piedmont. To these were added various territories in Italy, Germany, Holland and Catalonia. Here conscription applied, with local conscripts serving in numbered French units; new regiments formed after 1805 were entirely composed of foreigners. On occasion entire military organizations were embodied into the French Army. When Austria ceded parts of Croatia in the Treaty of Schönbrunn in 1809, Napoleon retained the Military Border institution intact, and in 1811 the six *Grenzer* regiments furnished three regiments, styled *Chasseurs d'Illyrie*, against Russia. Quite separate from these 'French' units were the foreign contingents. Napoleon was not inclined to turn away foreigners willing to fight and die for France. Under the Republic Bonaparte had used Polish and Italian volunteers, and the Empire enlisted a great variety of foreign units: Irish, Hanoverian, Portuguese, Prussian, Spanish, volunteer and prisoner-of-war groups freqenty formed and disbanded.

After 1805 the satellite states – Italy, Naples, Westphalia and the Grand Duchy of Poland – and the allied states of the Confederation of the Rhine provided additional manpower. The Confederation states were assigned troop quotas according to population, Bavaria furnishing the largest number – 30,000 men, with 110,000 serving in the campaigns between 1805 and 1813. Westphalia, a synthetic state created out of Hessian, Hanoverian and Prussian territories and ruled by Napoleon's brother Jerome, raised 70,000 soldiers out of a population of 2 million. Saxony, Württemberg and Baden each supplied substantial contingents. The Kingdom of Italy, with Napoleon's able stepson

Napoleonic conscription was based on legislation introduced by the Directoire. The annual recruit levy was based on quotas imposed on each department. The actual number called depended on the requirements of the army. Recruits received little formal instruction and normally were assigned directly to their regiments, marched to their destination in short stages, receiving uniforms, equipment, arms and training en route.

Eugène de Beauharnais as viceroy, provided a grand total of 121,000 men, and the Grand Duchy of Warsaw mustered 89,000 troops. The larger contingents formed separate corps with French commanders, while others served in composite formations. Generally they co-operated well with their French comrades and, except for the Neapolitans, were better than average soldiers. In the fall of 1813 the Germans became unreliable, but the Poles and the soldiers of the Kingdom of Italy remained loyal. The grand total for all the foreign contingents which at one time or the other served with Napoleon's armies came to 720,000 men. In 1812, including an Austrian and a Prussian auxiliary corps, they constituted over half of the 614,000 men assembled to invade Russia.

CHANGES WITHIN THE GRANDE ARMÉE

From 1807 the French Army changed. Never again was it able to train troops along the lines of the original Grande Armée. Experienced and capable officers became harder to find, the marshals became overly concerned with rewards and comforts, and even the emperor was no longer at the peak of his power. But if the change was decline, it should not be overstated. It certainly was not evident at Wagram, nor was it ever uniform throughout the army, especially in the Imperial Guard, to which Napoleon continued to add new units. The Middle Guard was formed in 1806; the Young Guard, the best of the annual recruit intake, was established in 1809.

No doubt French infantry was less capable of complex manoeuvres. To compensate, the emperor relied more on heavy formations requiring heavy skirmish screens. Nominally the designations of line and light were retained, but by 1808, except for minor differences in uniforms, distinctions between the two types disappeared in a trend towards an all-purpose arm. Artillery became ever more important. 'It is with artillery alone,' he told Bernadotte in 1806, 'that battles are won,' and repeated much the same in 1809. 'Fire alone is everything, the rest does not matter.' Despite the efforts made to increase the artillery establishment, the proportion of guns in the army only rose slowly to 3.5 per 1,000 in 1807–9. In part, this was due to efforts to phase out the 4-pounders and upgrade the throw weight of his field artillery because of the greater hitting power of heavy shot. The crucial bottleneck was the shortage of trained officers. Normally it took two years to train a gunnery officer, but in 1807 Napoleon decreed that junior officers could be produced in six months. 'There is no need that they know all about ballistics, all that is required is that they can serve in the field.'

THE FIRST PENINSULAR CAMPAIGNS

By late 1807 all continental European nations, except Denmark, Sweden and Portugal, had closed their ports to British commerce. But Britain retained access to Europe through the Iberian Peninsula, where Spain, allied with France since 1796, enforced the blockade loosely, and, after Trafalgar, had opened secret talks with London, while neutral Portugal maintained a lively trade with Britain. In June 1807 Napoleon demanded that Portugal and Denmark close their ports to British shipping. Britain countered by bombarding Copenhagen and seizing the Danish fleet, an example that kept Portugal from complying with Napoleon's demands.

In October 1807 he pressured the weak Spanish government to assist a 25,000-strong French army under General Junot to attack Portugal. The dual purpose of this expedition was to bring Portugal under French control and to introduce French troops into Spain. Although Spain co-operated in the unopposed operation, the march was difficult. Junot reached Lisbon on 1 December. With a 644-kilometre line of communications back to France, the occupation was viable only as long as Spain remained friendly. But Napoleon, unable to resist the temptation to meddle in the tangled affairs of the Spanish royal family, destroyed this arrangement. In early 1808, under the pretext of reinforcing Junot, Murat with 82,000 troops, second-line units for garrison and police duty only, occupied key fortresses in northern and central Spain, entering Madrid on 14 March. Napoleon now coerced the royal family to abdicate and in May installed his brother Joseph, until then king of Naples, as king of Spain. Murat, in turn, received the Neapolitan crown.

Initially there was little resistance, but French actions created popular resentment that exploded on 2 May in Madrid, brutally quelled by Murat. But the insurrection spread throughout the country. Provincial councils – *Juntas* – organized resistance forces, the Spanish troops marched home from Portugal and there were appeals for British support. Napoleon compounded his problems by dispersing his forces across Spain: one column was repulsed from Valencia, a second bogged down in a prolonged siege of Saragossa. Even worse, on 20 July 1808 a force of about 18,000 marching to take Cádiz was defeated and compelled to capitulate at Bailén. News of Bailén stunned Europe and ended the French reputation of invincibility. King Joseph, who had arrived in Madrid in June, hastily abandoned his capital and withdrew north of the Ebro river.

On 2 May 1808, aghast at the French occupation, the people of Madrid rose against the occupiers, but within a day the revolt was ferociously suppressed. Resistance to the French, however, soon spread and escalated throughout the country.

The Spanish insurrection gave England an opportunity to intervene on land. On 1 August a force of 15,000 men under Sir Arthur Wellesley, a young general who had made his reputation in India, landed in Portugal and defeated Junot at Vimeiro on 21 August, a victory negated when two superior officers agreed to transport the French back to France. A court of inquiry recalled all involved, leaving General Moore in command.

The events of the summer of 1808 were significant. Though by August the French in the Peninsula were reinforced to upward of 150,000 men, they had been thwarted by the combination of popular resistance with a small but effective British expeditionary force. Heartened by these developments Austria resolved to challenge France once again. Belatedly recognizing that Spain required major elements from the Grande Armée in Germany and that Austria was becoming a threat, Napoleon persuaded a reluctant Tsar Alexander to restrain Austria, and to deal with Spain. 'The war can be finished in a single operation but it must be properly co-ordinated and I must be there.' In November he assumed personal command. The Imperial Guard, three corps from Germany, the reserve cavalry, together with two Italian, one Polish and one German division, raised the Army of Spain to 305,000 with 250,000 effectives, which rapidly scattered the Spanish regulars in the north. Some regular formations survived in the south, but the Spanish Army was broken. Napoleon entered Madrid in December. He considered the war as good as over and expected the British to evacuate.

But Moore had moved north-eastwards into Spain to strike at Soult's isolated corps near Burgos. On 20 December Napoleon reacted, pushing north with Ney's corps to take Moore in the rear while Soult pinned him. In deep winter Moore retreated to Corunna where the Royal Navy took off his command on 16–17 January 1809, but the general was killed during the evacuation. By this time Napoleon, disturbed by reports about a conspiracy in Paris and Austrian mobilization, had already left Spain with his Guard. He would never return. Unfortunately he remained deluded on three important points: he underestimated the potential of a popular resistance movement supported by regular forces with a secure supply route; he believed that an army could feed itself in Spain; and finally he thought that communications and movement in Spain were easy. He did not establish a clear chain of command and did not hesitate to interfere from afar, ordering movements and operations as if this was the Lombard plain. So he handed over the conduct of the war to his brother and a group of fractious marshals. In May 1809, bringing reinforcements, Wellesley returned to Portugal.

RESHAPING THE HABSBURG ARMY

Following the débâcle of 1805, Archduke Charles was appointed Generalissimus, to command all forces in war and direct the military establishment in peace. His immediate objective was to improve the army's fighting capabilities, yet he was 'a conservative contending against soundly entrenched reactionaries [who] could never become fully reconciled to the techniques and to the energy and activity demanded by modern war'. His strategic perceptions did not break with the traditions of eighteenth-century war, but wavered between old and new concepts. In his manual for senior generals of the army, published in 1806, he wrote that war – a great evil – was 'governed by immutable laws ... based on irrefutable mathematical verities', and to terminate it as quickly as possible 'superior numbers should be concentrated at the decisive point'. But the manual insisted that commanders always protect communications and magazines and, silent with regard to initiative expected of senior commanders, its emphasis on supply, careful planning and precise alignments in battle inhibited flexibility and enterprise.

Corps formations, nine 'line' and two reserve corps, were only activated during mobilization in February 1809. The line corps had three divisions: one designated as the advance guard, composed entirely of light troops, the others each with two or three infantry brigades.

Reserve corps were formed by combining the heavy cavalry and Grenadier battalions. The larger I Reserve Corps had twelve grenadier battalions and six heavy cavalry regiments; II Reserve Corps had about half this number. Corps, averaging about 29,000 men, fought as compact bodies, rarely deployed on a frontage exceeding 3 kilometres, and could be directed by an energetic commander with an efficient staff. The emperor, however, reserved the right to make senior appointments and, in 1809, corps commanders were selected by birth and seniority rather than by merit. This demanded more from their staffs, but, lacking training and common doctrine, these officers were incapable of handling the corps system effectively, and were hampered by constant interference from the archduke's staff. Yet the corps system provided greater staying power and, even when defeated, the army managed to extricate itself without total disaster.

Tactics remained antiquated. The 1807 infantry regulations emphasized the three-deep line, columns were permitted for attack and a closed battalion column, capable of moving in the face of hostile cavalry, was introduced. The number of skirmishers was increased but their actions tightly controlled. Austrian horse continued to charge in a two-deep line, a poor formation against the compact columns of the French mounted arm. Artillery was reorganized. The regimental pieces were grouped into eight-gun brigade batteries, while heavier guns were assigned to the tactical control of chiefs of artillery at corps and army level, providing more concentrated firepower when needed.

Charles opposed militias as politically unreliable, while creating the illusion that they disposed of 'large masses of combatants and induced a false sense of security'. Realizing that 'after fifteen years of fighting ... and misfortune' the state could not sustain an enlarged regular establishment, in the late spring of 1808 he reluctantly agreed to the formation of a *Landwehr*. Enrolling all males aged 18 to 45 in Austria and Bohemia, on paper the organization mustered 180,000 men, though its combat value remained in doubt.

THE WAR OF 1809: THE RATISBON PHASE

There was little co-ordination between Austrian diplomacy and military planning. Diplomats were certain that Russia would remain neutral and that Prussia would honour a provisional agreement to assist Austria with 80,000 men. But in March 1809 the cautious Prussian king repudiated his undertaking even though London promised funds and a major diversionary operation in north-western Europe. Finally, there were hopes for nationalist revolts in Germany. Mobilization began in January and on 8 February 1809 a crown council reaffirmed the decision for war. By this time, however, Charles had lost confidence because, as he later wrote, 'our chances for success were minimal'. He had doubts about the corps system and the war plan, and, though personally brave, was overawed by Napoleon.

Austria's best chance for victory was an early offensive in Germany. The shortest line of operations was the valley of the Danube from Vienna to Strassburg, but, because Prussian co-operation was still expected, and also to divide French forces in Germany, a more northerly approach, the Main valley, was chosen. Army headquarters and five line and one reserve corps assembled in Bohemia, while one line and the smaller reserve corps deployed along the Inn. Italy, now a secondary theatre, was assigned to Archduke John's two-corps Army of Inner Austria, forming in Carinthia and Carniola. Finally, near Cracow, there was Archduke Ferdinand with one corps. Adding various detachments, field forces numbered 283,401 men with 742 field guns in 108 batteries, backed by 312,000 depot, reserve and *Landwehr* troops.

The French and allied forces in Germany, weakened by withdrawals for Spain, were slowly getting ready. In December Napoleon established the Army of the Rhine and ordered the approximately 60,000 French troops in Germany to concentrate around Nuremberg and Ratisbon, while instructing the Confederation states to mobilize. From Paris Napoleon took additional measures. He sent Berthier to Germany as acting commander and recalled Marshals Lannes, Lefebvre, and Bessières from Spain. The emperor expected war, but he did not expect hostilities to start until May. French concentration was not complete by the end of March. Davout's strong III Corps was moving towards Ratisbon, while Massena with IV Corps was moving from Frankfurt and Strasburg into Bavaria. Other French and allied contingents were mustering, but would not become available until the end of May. Command arrangements were poor. Visual telegraph communications between Napoleon in Paris and Berthier in Bavaria failed, and, in the second week of April, Davout's right wing north of Ratisbon was still separated by 100 kilometres from Massena, the gap covered by Lefebvre's VII Corps – 30,000 Bavarians.

If Charles had struck late in March he would have caught the French off balance and perhaps gained victories which might have induced Prussia to abandon her neutrality. But he hesitated. Apprehensive that the French might mass on the Danube to advance on Vienna, while his advance west from Bohemia was difficult and the heads of column might be attacked as they emerged from the Bohemian mountains, he shifted his line of operations south of the Danube. On 13 March, leaving behind two corps, the Austrian Army moved south. The three weeks required for the move delayed the Austrian offensive, enabled Napoleon to take personal command and rally his forces, while Charles exhausted his troops and divided his army. The two corps left behind under General Bellegarde in Bohemia served no useful purpose. The transfer completed in the first week of April, Charles ordered hostilities to commence on 10 April. A war manifesto distributed to the troops – 'Europe looks for freedom under your banners … your German brethren wait for redemption at your hands' – had little appeal to the soldiers and failed to impress Napoleon's German allies.

The slow Austrian advance created operational problems. To sunder the enemy before he could concentrate, Ingolstadt had to be reached in eight marches. But hampered by a large train and poor staff work, the army only reached Landshut, 65 kilometres north-east of Munich, on 16 April. Bellegarde also made little progress. Lacking precise information about the location of the enemy, Napoleon ordered

THE WAR OF 1809

Encouraged by events in Spain and the reorganization of its army Austria, though without allies and with a hostile Russia in its rear, went to war against Napoleon on 10 April 1809. An attempt to defeat the dispersed Army of Germany failed after Napoleon defeated Archduke Charles in a series of battles around Ratisbon and

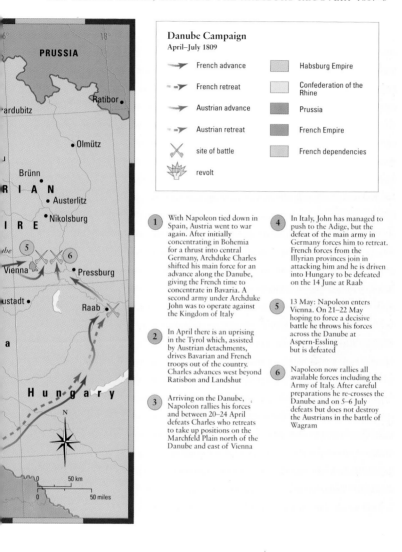

Danube Campaign
April–July 1809

→ French advance

--→ French retreat

→ Austrian advance

--→ Austrian retreat

⚔ site of battle

revolt

Habsburg Empire

Confederation of the Rhine

Prussia

French Empire

French dependencies

PRUSSIA

Ratibor

ardubitz

Olmütz

Brünn

R I A N

Austerlitz

I R E   Nikolsburg

5   6

Vienna   Pressburg

ustadt

Raab

H u n g a r y

N

0   50 km

0   50 miles

1 With Napoleon tied down in Spain, Austria went to war again. After initially concentrating in Bohemia for a thrust into central Germany, Archduke Charles shifted his main force for an advance along the Danube, giving the French time to concentrate in Bavaria. A second army under Archduke John was to operate against the Kingdom of Italy

2 In April there is an uprising in the Tyrol which, assisted by Austrian detachments, drives Bavarian and French troops out of the country. Charles advances west beyond Ratisbon and Landshut

3 Arriving on the Danube, Napoleon rallies his forces and between 20–24 April defeats Charles who retreats to take up positions on the Marchfeld Plain north of the Danube and east of Vienna

4 In Italy, John has managed to push to the Adige, but the defeat of the main army in Germany forces him to retreat. French forces from the Illyrian provinces join in attacking him and he is driven into Hungary to be defeated on the 14 June at Raab

5 13 May: Napoleon enters Vienna. On 21–22 May hoping to force a decisive battle he throws his forces across the Danube at Aspern-Essling but is defeated

6 Napoleon now rallies all available forces including the Army of Italy. After careful preparations he re-crosses the Danube and on 5–6 July defeats but does not destroy the Austrians in the battle of Wagram

compelled him to withdraw just east of Vienna to positions on the Marchfeld. After initial success in Italy, Archduke John was driven back into Hungary. Wavering between hope and despair, Archduke Charles fought the battles of Aspern–Essling, 21–22 May, a tactical victory, and Wagram, 5–6 July, a qualified defeat.

Davout to occupy Ratisbon. On 17 April Charles decided to move north to link up with Bellegarde; the next day, realizing Davout's vulnerable position, Charles advanced to attack him, leaving one corps to protect his left flank. But Napoleon had arrived at army headquarters on 17 April and recognized the threat. He pulled Davout out of Ratisbon to combine with Lefebvre east of Ingolstadt. Lannes, newly arrived from Spain, was to form a provisional corps; Massena and Oudinot were urged to hurry. 'Activity, activity, speed, I greet you,' the emperor told Massena.

Napoleon judged the series of battles in Bavaria, 20–24 April, among his most brilliant operations. With Davout and Lefebvre acting as a holding force, Lannes and Massena would attack the Austrian centre and left wing. The actions of 21 April – a series of encounters along a 45-kilometre front collectively known as the battle of Abensberg – pushed the Austrian left wing back beyond Landshut. Here Napoleon discovered that the bulk of the enemy army had moved north against Davout. Before dawn the next day Napoleon, with 40,000 men under Massena and Lannes, started north, and in the early afternoon he brought off another *manoeuvre sur les derrières* when Lannes's columns crashed into the Austrian left flank at Eggmühl. That night Charles withdrew the bulk of his army north of the Danube, informing the Emperor Francis that peace had become imperative. The army, he wrote, 'had to be saved at any price' because it might 'be needed to deal with internal problems'.

In the Ratisbon campaign Napoleon, with a hastily assembled army, had wrested the initiative from the Austrians who had revealed grave shortcomings in command and control. The staff had failed to regulate movements and corps commanders had displayed little initiative, in part because Charles did not give them much discretion and rarely informed them of his plans. Also, there was a tendency to hold too many troops in reserve. Charles had engaged only half of his command, the rest standing to arms but contributing little. Even so, the corps structure had enabled the army to escape destruction.

THE ASPERN–ESSLING PHASE

The change in the fortunes of the main army compelled all other Austrian forces to assume the defensive. In Italy Archduke John's Army of Inner Austria had pushed Eugène's army back to the Adige, but was recalled to join the main army. By mid May, defeated on the Piave, he retreated into Inner Austria, and after Marmont's corps from Dalmatia had reinforced Eugène, he was driven east into Hungary. In Poland Archduke Ferdinand had advanced to Warsaw but now had to fall back into Galicia. In the Tyrol the regulars who had supported the mountaineers to expel Bavarian garrisons were withdrawn, though the Tyroleans fought on even after Austria made peace in October. But apart from diverting some Bavarian and a few French troops, the revolt had no strategic consequences. And Charles's appeal to German nationalism had largely fallen flat. The spring and summer of 1809 saw a succession of armed risings in Westphalia and Brunswick. The Prussian Major Friedrich von Schill led his troopers to support Hanoverian resistance, but was driven into Stralsund on 28 May by Dutch and Danish troops. Schill was killed fighting, his captured officers shot and his men sent to the galleys. The Duke of Brunswick-Oels and his 'Black Hussars' were luckier. They invaded Saxony and occupied Dresden in June, and after Austria's defeat fought their way to the North Sea where British ships rescued them. Militarily these exploits had only nuisance value, but they contributed to the rising sense of German nationalism.

The decisive battles were fought north of the Danube and east of Vienna. Napoleon had marched east along the south bank of the Danube, pursuing the Austrian left wing commanded by Hiller, while keeping Charles and the Army of Inner Austria divided. Discovering that, except for some volunteer units, the *Landwehr* was unwilling to fight, Hiller conducted a delaying action on 3 May at Ebelsberg, then crossed to the north bank of the Danube on 11 May to join the main body. Once again, the Austrians did not defend Vienna, but evacuated on 12 May, abandoning vast magazines.

By 17 May Charles had assembled his army on the Marchfeld plain, 15 kilometres east of Vienna, on the north bank of the Danube that was then divided into several branches and at flood stage. Approximately 18 kilometres wide and 13 deep, the Marchfeld was dotted with small villages, including Aspern and Essling on the water's edge. Its main feature was the Russbach brook at its northern edge, behind which the

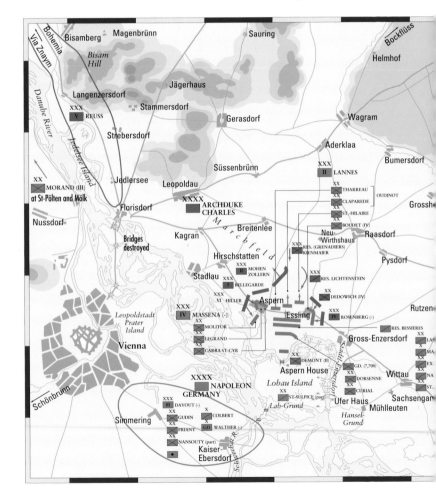

ground rose to form a low escarpment with the villages of Wagram and Markgrafneusiedl on its ridgeline. To the north-west the plateau merged into a range of hills.

Incorporating Hiller's troops and the Vienna garrison, but detaching strong formations to guard his flanks, Charles had 95,800 troops and 264 guns available for battle. While corps designation remained, he had reverted to the traditional order of battle, fighting the army in the traditional multi-columns and three-wing order. There was now a single army advance guard, while the two reserve corps were consolidated into a Grenadier and a Cavalry Corps. Despite pressure to attack the French at once – at this point Napoleon had only 82,000 men – the archduke refused to venture across a broad river in flood. He knew Napoleon would have to attack him and did not intend to fight at the water's edge, so he allowed the enemy to transfer substantial forces and attack him when he was getting ready to debouch into the plain beyond.

The archduke surmised correctly. Afraid that the Austrians might retreat out of reach, Napoleon wanted an early battle. Reconnaissance found a crossing point downstream from Vienna where the large Lobau Island and several smaller sand bars provided an opportunity to site bridges on to the

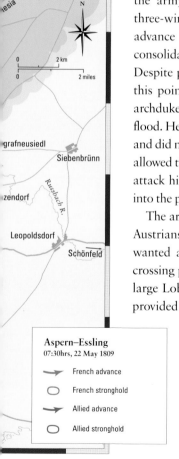

Aspern–Essling
07:30hrs, 22 May 1809

→ French advance
◯ French stronghold
→ Allied advance
◯ Allied stronghold

ASPERN–ESSLING 21–22 MAY 1809
Although only a tactical victory that Charles refused to follow up, Austrian fighting qualities impressed Napoleon who told Murat later, 'you did not see the Austrians at Aspern, therefore you have not seen anything.'

Marchfeld. Lobau Island was seized on 18 May and engineers constructed a series of flimsy bridges to the far side, the final link 225 metres long, from the Lobau to the north shore between Aspern on the left and Essling on the right. The bridges were completed on 20 May, and light cavalry and an infantry division crossed to establish a lodgement. By midnight Massena and the rest of his corps, followed by Bessières and the Guard cavalry, were across. By this time rising waters and a series of hulks floated downstream by the Austrians had twice broken the bridges, but, by mid-morning on 21 May, 23,000 men – three infantry, two cavalry divisions – were deployed in the bridgehead area. Infantry occupied the two villages with cavalry in the interval.

Archduke Charles, his forces posted in six columns between Wagram and the Danube, ordered a concentric attack against the French at 10 a.m., but poor timing negated Austrian numerical superiority. With Massena in Aspern and Lannes in Essling, the French lost only a part of Aspern, and, despite another breach in the bridge, Napoleon reinforced his troops during the afternoon and the night. By early on 22 May Napoleon, now on the north bank, had doubled his forces with the arrival of the rest of Lannes's II Corps, the Guard infantry and additional cavalry. At sunrise the French retook all of Aspern while the Essling garrison repulsed an Austrian dawn assault. Although Davout's corps had not yet arrived, at about 7 a.m. Napoleon decided to break the Austrian centre. Three divisions of II Corps, supported by cavalry, advanced. Initially the attack made good progress, but stalled when Charles in person rallied his troops. About then, Napoleon, informed that the bridge had been wrecked again, ordered a pull back to the Aspern–Essling line. Austrian grenadiers took most of Essling except for the stone-built granary. After the Young Guard retook the village in the afternoon, the emperor ordered a withdrawal to Lobau Island that proceeded in good order. Curiously, Austrian pressure eased as the rearguard fell back to the bridge and then to the Lobau. Losses had been heavy. The Austrians lost 5,200 dead and 21,500 wounded, the French about the same. As usual, French senior officer casualties were heavier than the Austrian. Besides Marshal Lannes, who later died of his wounds, three generals fell in action and eighteen were wounded, against one Austrian general killed and thirteen senior officers wounded.

There was no pursuit, not even a bombardment of the troop-crammed island. Essentially Charles had fought a defensive battle to exhaust and debilitate the enemy, but lacked the desire to destroy him. His success was not due to brilliant strategy but to his own bravery and the courage of his troops against an enemy who had gambled. Charles hoped that his tactical victory would push Prussia and Russia to join Austria, and that fear of such developments would induce Napoleon to make peace. Napoleon, however, was made of sterner stuff. He refused to order evacuation of the Lobau and rejected a pull-back to Vienna. He recognized that the Austrians had fought well, but asserted that the rising Danube had defeated his army. He was determined to try again and made sure that neither the Danube nor inferior numbers would ruin his next attempt.

On 21–22 May 1809 Archduke Charles achieved the first setback against Napoleon in person, fighting a French attempt to strike across the Danube to a hold in a small bridgehead. This picture shows Charles, a man of substantial personal courage, on the morning of the second day after having steadied his troops and thrown back a determined French attack.

Napoleon converted the Lobau and several adjacent islands into fire bases mounting 129 heavy guns, had a strong barrier placed upriver in the Danube to protect four new bridges to the Lobau, and prepared to throw ten pontoon bridges from there to the north bank. Redoubts and a flotilla of ten gunboats secured the island bases against Austrian attacks. Finally, Napoleon summoned all available troops for battle, raising his strength to almost 178,000 men. This included the Lobau garrisons, IX (Saxon) Corps under Bernadotte and the Army of Italy that on 14 June had defeated John's Army of Inner Austria at Raab, and had driven it into Pressburg on the north bank of the Danube. Moving up were Lefebvre's Bavarians.

Curiously, Charles did little to improve his position. He rejected suggestions to strike across the river and continued imploring the emperor to seek peace. Meanwhile, his army received few reinforcements, mainly

Repulsed at Aspern–Essling, Napoleon made careful preparations. Building strong bridges, he turned Lobau Island into a powerful fire base and a vast assembly area. Here, between 2 and 4 July 1809, artillery and cavalry are crossing over the southern branch of the Danube to their concentration areas.

Landwehr units, which he brigaded with regulars, making the total 130,000 men with 414 guns. His brother John ignored repeated appeals to join him with his army, but in any case that command now numbered a mere 12,000 men. Charles meanwhile constructed a series of badly designed and sited redoubts in the plain opposite the Lobau, though he did little to fortify the Russbach line. Above all, he failed to develop a coherent battle plan. He wavered between meeting the enemy on the water's edge or letting him advance on to the plain, where, when he was pinned against the Russbach, he would attack and destroy him in a double envelopment. In the end he made a poor compromise. Hiller's corps and the Advance Guard were to delay the enemy on the Aspern–Essling line, retard his progress and buy time for the main body to take up positions. After arguing for several days that his weak corps could not possibly accomplish this assignment, on 4 July Hiller took leave. While his assessment was correct, his action underlined the self-centred feuding which impaired the functions of the Austrian high command. Charles, of course, had made a mistake. Fewer troops could have observed the enemy,

the heavy French batteries blew apart the redoubts, and, brushed aside, the forward elements suffered heavy casualties unnecessarily.

On 4 July the Lobau batteries began to bombard the Austrian redoubts, demolishing the works. Heavy thunderstorms throughout the afternoon and night helped to hide the French crossing of the Danube. Berthier's meticulous planning paid off. Early on 5 July major elements of three corps, rising by afternoon to six corps, the Guard and the cavalry reserve were deployed on the plain. The Austrians had been pushed back and by evening the French right – Bernadotte, Eugène, Oudinot and Davout – faced the Russbach,

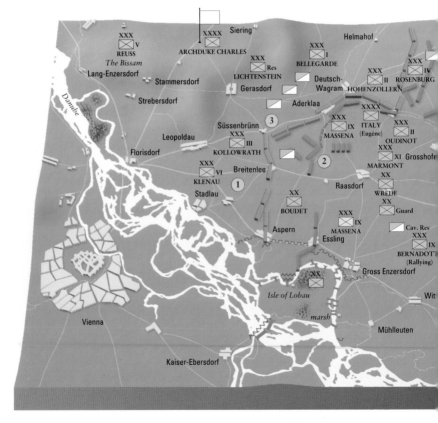

Massena covered the left centre, the Imperial Guard and the cavalry were in reserve, Marmont and one Bavarian division were crossing. As light was fading Napoleon launched a hasty attack on the Russbach positions – it failed. When combat ended at about ten that night the Austrians, fighting on good defensive ground and resolutely led, had outfought the enemy.

His confidence restored, Charles issued orders for a general attack soon after sunrise the next day. The weak French left wing along the Danube was to be driven in by a two-corps *manoeuvre sur les derrières*, while along the Russbach three infantry and one cavalry corps were to advance simultaneously. It was a bold plan, with success depending on exact timing. With orders only going out after 2 a.m. on 6 July to corps deployed in a 23-kilometre arc, this clearly was impossible. In the event Davout contained the Austrian left, but in the centre Bernadotte's poorly handled Saxon corps was routed. A furious Napoleon dismissed the marshal on the spot. Because of delayed orders the attack against

grafneusiedl
X
III
OUT
zendorf
Russbach
Leopoldsdorf
XX

NAPOLEON

XXXX
ARCHDUKE JOHN
(still approaching)

THE BATTLE OF WAGRAM, 5–6 JULY 1809

Archduke Charles's plan to envelop Napoleon on the plain failed, but Napoleon had to resort to an unprecedented heavy bombardment and large columns to break into the Austrian line.

1 During the morning of the 5 July Archduke Charles launches an attack on Napoleon's left wing in order to seize the bridges across the Danube. The attack was halted by Massena's corps.

2 6 July: Napoleon concentrates his forces and artillery, the greatest concentration of artillery to date on the Austrian centre, while Davout's corps attack the Austrian left

3 The Austrian centre is penetrated and the left flank pushed back, Archduke Charles orders a phase withdrawal towards the northeast

the weakly held extreme French left wing came three hours late, but made good progress towards the bridges where it stalled under heavy fire from the Lobau batteries. Meanwhile, French cavalry filled the gap supported by a 112-gun grand battery, and Massena disengaged from the centre, marched across the Austrian front and restored the situation on the left, while Macdonald's corps of the Army of Italy filled the gap. Charles's ambitious plan had failed.

On the right Davout was making progress around Markgraf-neusiedl, while Napoleon ordered Macdonald to break the Austrian centre west of the Russbach. After a heavy bombardment Macdonald advanced in a huge hollow 8,000-strong square, taking enormous casualties, but reinforced by a Bavarian division and the Young Guard which pressed on. By this time Davout was winning the battle. Shortly after noon he turned the Austrian left and threatened to roll up the Russbach line. Having lost hope that John's army would arrive, at 2.30 in the afternoon Charles issued orders for a phased withdrawal. The French were too weary to pursue and the Austrians got away in fair order with about 80,000 men, including one corps Charles had held in reserve, still combat capable. With over 320,000 men engaged, Napoleon had won the largest battle fought in Europe. But the cost had been heavy: some 70,000 casualties divided almost evenly between both sides.

Although the French failed to pursue until late on 7 July, Charles had lost heart. Retreating into Moravia he fought a few brief engagements but then asked for an armistice on 11 July and resigned his command when the emperor, still hoping for English, Prussian or even Russian intervention, refused to accept the need for immediate peace. The promised British landing in late July, in Holland not Germany, failed, and on 14 October Austria had to sign the Peace of Schönbrunn, losing Salzburg to Bavaria, the Illyrian Provinces to Napoleon and parts of Galicia to the Grand Duchy of Warsaw and to Russia. In addition she had to pay a huge indemnity, limit her army to 150,000 and rejoin the Continental System.

WAGRAM ANALYSED

It is commonplace to say that Wagram marked a decline in the capabilities of Napoleon's infantry and therefore he had to use artillery and heavy columns instead of rapid manoeuvre by highly motivated and trained troops. Yet matters were not that simple. Of course, this was no longer the army that had marched out of Boulogne in 1805, and training standards had declined. But the fighting qualities of his troops were high, if only because less experienced troops often fought more aggressively than veterans who had acquired survival skills. The combat performance of Davout's and Massena's corps was equal to anything in the past, indeed all corps fought well. Italians and Bavarians matched French performance at Wagram, and the Saxons did very well on the first day and routed on the second because of Bernadotte's poor leadership. As for commanders, the marshals, except for Bernadotte, did well and for once, given the distances on the battlefield, were given a great deal of tactical initiative. The French army at Wagram had changed but hardly declined.

As for the Austrians, the troops had done more than their duty. Napoleon, in a good position to judge, reprimanded those who belittled them by stating more than once, 'it is obvious that you were not at Wagram'. But Archduke Charles lost much of his lustre. His reorganization of artillery had worked, but his system of command and control had failed. His relations with senior commanders were poor. He did not reveal his overall plan of battle to his subordinates and deprived them of initiative. His envelopment scheme for the second day of battle was unrealistic, taking no account of the time and distance required to transmit and execute his orders. Above all, he was too cautious a commander and too concerned with preserving the army to rate as a truly great commander.

The war of 1809 was less brilliant perhaps than the amazing campaigns of 1805, yet, for the time being, Napoleon and his army still dominated the continent. However, there remained Spain, the famous 'ulcer' gnawing away at his dominance.

CHAPTER FIVE

The Peninsular War: Wellington and the Guerrillas 1809–13

Field Marshal Sir Arthur Wellesley, Duke of Wellington, was one of the outstanding soldiers of his age. Here shown in full dress uniform, he generally dressed modestly, well below his military station, preferring a practical grey frock coat worn with a low-cocked hat, comfortable half boots and a dark cloak to the gaudier dress worn by his French opponents.

The Peninsular War:
Wellington and the Guerrillas

NAPOLEON HAD INTENDED TO return to Spain after Wagram, boasting that 'when I appear beyond the Pyrenees, the terrified Leopard [England] will seek the ocean to avoid shame, defeat and death', but he never returned. For the next two years he remained in Paris, preoccupied with his marriage to Marie-Louise – the daughter of Emperor Francis – the birth of an heir and administrative concerns. These were weighty matters, but Iberia was more so. Napoleon greatly underestimated the operational problems there. He would have been wise to abandon such an exposed position, but, because he believed that even a limited retreat would have grave repercussions in Europe, he would not withdraw from Spain or even reposition his forces behind the Ebro line.

In 1810 Wellesley, later the Duke of Wellington, analysed the basic strategic problem facing the French. 'They must employ a very large force indeed in the operations which will render it necessary for us to go away; and I doubt whether they can bring that force to bear upon Portugal without abandoning other objects and exposing their whole fabric in France to great risk.' By 1810 an effective resistance movement functioned in the mountain areas where guerrilla bands, supported by surviving regular units, attacked French garrisons, convoys, outposts and Spanish collaborators. Still, the French troops – a mix of French, Polish, Italian, Swiss and German – controlled most of the country except for besieged Cádiz and some areas in Aragón, Valencia and Galicia. Wellington realized that his forces alone could not recover the country, but held that even though the Spanish armies might be routed 'the war of the partisans may continue'. Thus the guerrilla bands and the Anglo-Portuguese armies were interdependent. Without the presence of Wellington's regulars the French probably could have crushed or at least contained the bands, and if the French had not been diverted by the guerrillas the Anglo-Portuguese might well have been unable to withstand a concentrated French attack.

WELLINGTON'S ARMY

The British Army in the Peninsula was much changed from the indifferent forces expelled from the continent in 1795. Between 1795 and 1809 the British Army greatly improved its capabilities, though compared to continental armies the regular forces of the Crown remained small, retaining the character of the professional bodies of the eighteenth century. Officers were drawn largely from the lesser aristocracy and gentry. Normal promotion was by seniority rather than merit, a slow process at best, but a wealthy man, as long as he had served a minimum time in rank, could purchase his next promotion. Usually these men were brave and increasingly competent, but, except for the artillery and the engineers, none had any formal training. Insalubrious climate and war created a high casualty rate and this speeded advancement and even allowed promotion from the ranks: about one officer in twenty was so promoted. From 1792 there was a permanent commander-in-chief, an office held from 1795 to 1809 by the reform-minded Duke of York – an indifferent field commander but a fine administrator who mitigated the worst abuses of the purchase system and worked to improve training and humanize discipline. His efforts to increase efficiency and rationalize administration were attacked by all sides in Parliament, which throughout the conflict jealously guarded its supremacy, even at the cost of military efficiency.

Despite a decade and a half fighting French mass armies, Britain refused to introduce conscription. Replacements and additional manpower were found by voluntary enlistment, especially in Ireland where destitution was so great that the bounty and the prospect of rations were powerful inducements. But with pickings slimmer in England and Scotland the government increasingly relied on various Army Reserve Acts passed between 1802 and 1811, to encourage transfers from the militia. The result was that the rank and file grew from about 45,000 in

French Empire
1810

- under direct rule by Napoleon
- under rule by members of Napoleon's family
- dependent state

NORWAY
Christiana
Shetland Is.
Stockholm
SWEDEN
Gothenburg

North Sea

Edinburgh

DENMARK
Copenhagen

UNITED KINGDOM
OF GREAT BRITAIN
AND IRELAND
Dublin

Helgoland
1807–14 to Br.
to Sweden
Hamburg
PRUSS
1807–10
to Fr.
Brandenburg
Berlin
WESTPHALIA
Erfurt

Amsterdam
1810 to Fr.
London
Antwerp
Brussels Cologne
Prague
Bohemia
Frankfurt

0   200 km
0   200 miles

Channel Is.

Paris

Orléans

Tours

FRANCE

Bern
HELVETIA
Geneva
1798–1814 to Fr.
Lyon
Milan
Turin
ITALY
Venice

CONFEDERATION
OF THE RHINE
Munich
Vienna
Styria
Carinth

Illyrian Provinc

ATLANTIC OCEAN

Bordeaux

Toulouse
Marseille

LUCCA
Florence
Tuscany

Adri

Cataloña
1808–13 to Fr.
Barcelona

Corsica

Papal
States
Rome

Oporto

Madrid

PORTUGAL

SPAIN

Lisbon

Balearic Is.

SARDINIA

NAP

Naples

Mediterranean Sea

Palermo

SICILY

Gibraltar
to Spain
Ceuta
to Spain

MOROCCO

Oran

Algiers

ALGERIA

Bona

Tunis

Tunisia

M

1800

THE GRAND EMPIRE

In 1810 Napoleon dominated Europe as no ruler before him. France had almost doubled in size since 1789 including Belgium. Holland, western and northern Germany, Italy including Piedmont, Genoa, the Papal States and the Illyrian Provinces. Beyond were the satellite kingdoms of Italy, Naples, Spain, and Westphalia.

1793 to 200,000 by 1809 and 330,000 in 1813. The great majority of troops were long-service volunteers, mostly uneducated and including many social misfits, kept under control by application of the lash. Convinced that only brutal punishments could control his men – 'all enlisted for drink' he maintained – Wellington did not agree with reform-minded officers such as Moore that discipline based on leadership and mutual respect would bring out the best from the rank and file. This type of discipline was tried in the new, partly rifle-armed, light troops Moore had trained in 1804–5. The Light Division, combining light troops and the rifle regiments, came to be regarded as the élite formation in the Peninsula, but even here flogging was applied and overall the army retained its draconian discipline.

Numbers had increased, but with well over half of the army deployed in distant parts, actual troop commitments on the continent remained small. The number of British soldiers in the Peninsula never exceeded 40,000, inclusive of the fine regiments of the King's German Legion (KGL), and supported by the British-trained Portuguese Army. Battalions, cavalry regiments and batteries formed into divisions constituted the basic fighting elements; corps formations were only introduced in 1811. The pattern of a small field force, supported by foreign auxiliaries, continued until the very end. When Wellington faced Napoleon at Waterloo only 31,000 officers and men of his 67,000-strong army were British.

Given the continued numerical superiority of the French, security of his Portuguese base had to be Wellesley's highest priority and his initial strategy was defensive. His greatest assets were his short supply line back to the coast, while that of the French extended all the way back to France, and the guerrillas who made it impossible for the French to concentrate their scattered forces for a continuing campaign. He was a master in the organization of marches and supplies and took great pains to feed his army, not only because the poverty of the country demanded it, but also to keep his men as controlled as possible. After Napoleon withdrew troops from Spain in 1812 Wellington went on the offensive, repeatedly defeating French forces in battle. The following year, reinforced and finally in command of all British and allied troops, he began operations that drove the enemy north of the Ebro, culminating in the climactic battle of Vitoria on 21 June 1813, which for all purposes ended the French presence in Spain.

The mainstay of Wellington's army was his well-trained infantry. It retained linear tactics, but reduced battalion battle lines to two ranks. A master of tactics, the Duke usually, although not always, chose to fight on the defensive. He would look for a position with secure flanks and shelter his troops out of sight on the reverse slope of a ridge. Only the British guns remained on the crest. His numerous light infantry, one-fifth of his total – rifle-armed specialists from the Light Division, light battalions of the King's German Legion, Portuguese *Cacadores* (sharpshooters) and light companies from the line battalions – deployed well forward down the front slopes to contest the advance of the enemy light infantry. Denied exact knowledge of Wellington's precise position, his adversaries might blunder into his line without proper deployment. Concealed until the French topped the crest, the British line infantry would fire one or two close-range volleys, followed up by a controlled bayonet charge which usually hurled the enemy back.

The other combat arms – artillery and cavalry – were not as fully integrated as Napoleon's. British artillery was highly competent, though always inferior to the French in the number of guns and weight of metal. In the Peninsula the British were usually short of field artillery, and would distribute guns along the battle line to augment infantry fire. Despite their professionalism, or rather because of it, the anti-intellectual Wellington disliked gunnery officers. He did approve of the gentlemanly cavalry officers, but until 1812 never had more than 2,000 troopers at his disposal. Also, this arm, though proficient in horsemanship and effective in mounted charges, displayed an exasperating tendency to charge out of control. The exception, of course, was the great charge at Salamanca where General LeMarchant handled his 7,000 sabres with great skill.

British industry, emerging from the early Industrial Revolution, hit its full stride after 1808. The Royal Navy, the army and, increasingly, the Allies were supplied by the growing output of weapons, equipment and munitions, with British gunpowder considered the best available. Curiously, neither Napoleon, Wellington nor indeed any major commander had much interest in new technology. None the less, British artillery introduced two technological innovations during the conflict. The first was shrapnel – named after its inventor Lieutenant Shrapnel, Royal Artillery – a hollow shell containing musket balls and explosives, doubling the range of canister. Given to premature explosions, its effectiveness was disputed, though Wellington pronounced it 'a great benefit'. By contrast, he was little impressed by the rockets developed by Sir William Congreve and issued in 1806. With payloads up to 15 kilograms, these unguided missiles were launched from wheeled frames or copper troughs mounted on tripods. They lacked accuracy and were most effective in area bombardment. Wellington disliked them. 'I do not,' he remarked, 'want to set fire to any town.'

BRITISH ALLIED AND AUXILIARY FORCES

Then, as later, British soldiers showed their habitual disdain for foreigners. During the early campaigns in Flanders they had disliked the Dutch, while encounters with Russian soldiers and sailors during the abortive expedition to North Holland in 1799 produced little in the way of good feeling. It was during the Peninsular campaign that the British came into the most prolonged and intimate contact with foreign allies, and relations here were poor most of the time. Both Moore and Wellington considered the Spaniards poor fighters. Wellington, in particular, was often disappointed with Spanish commanders. The

From May 1808 on, the guerrilla war in most areas of Spain was conducted with great brutality and countless atrocities on both sides. In this drawing by Goya, Spanish peasants armed only with sharpened stakes and knives are attacking French soldiers armed with muskets and bayonets.

sentiment that the Spaniards were 'never to be relied upon in the moment of trial and danger' was widely shared by his officers and men. British resentments were only partially justified. The surviving Spanish regular armies, cobbled together from remaining regular units and local militias, marched from one unsuccessful battle to the next. After his early experiences with their performance Wellington lacked confidence in them. However, the Spanish government, such as it was, needed an army if only as a symbol of national existence. When broken, the regulars provided useful reinforcements for the organized and increasingly effective guerrilla bands which, from 1810 on, took over the war against the French from the popular insurrections. Nevertheless, the British, who often fraternized with the French between battles, were appalled by the atrocities committed by the Spanish and Portuguese irregulars against the French and their Spanish collaborators. Relations were better with the Portuguese Army, reconstituted after 1809 by Major General Beresford assisted by a British cadre. From 1810 Portuguese regiments were often brigaded with British divisions.

The most congenial among the British foreign units was the King's German Legion, originally formed from Hanoverian soldiers who had escaped when their army had capitulated in 1803. Part of the armed forces of the Crown, uniformed and equipped on the English pattern, the KGL expanded eventually to 18,000 all arms and was considered as good as the best British units. It took part in almost every British expedition to the continent and continued as part of the British Army until 1816.

THE WAR IN THE PENINSULA: THE DEFENCE OF PORTUGAL
When Wellesley returned in late April 1809 his command numbered just 28,000 British and about 16,000 Portuguese troops, while the French Army of Spain mustered 360,000 men, though many were tied up in garrisons and along the line of communications. Immediately, Wellesley faced Soult in northern Portugal and King Joseph in Spain

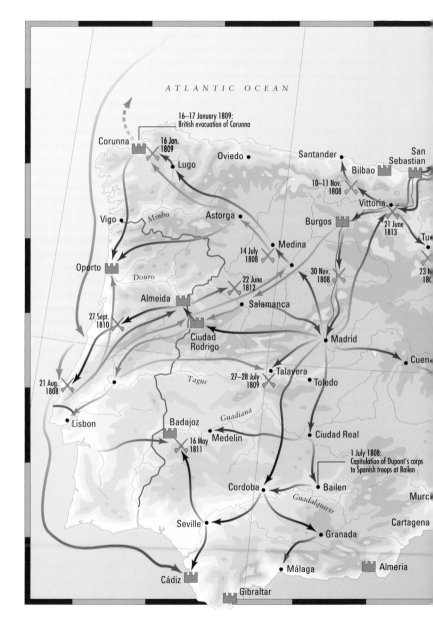

ATLANTIC OCEAN

16–17 January 1809:
British evacuation of Corunna

Corunna
16 Jan.
1809
Lugo
Oviedo
Santander
San
Sebastian
Bilbao
10–11 Nov.
1808
Vittoria
Vigo
Minho
Astorga
Burgos
21 June
1813
Tu
Medina
14 July
1808
30 Nov.
1808
23 N
18(
Oporto
Douro
22 June
1812
Almeida
Salamanca
27 Sept.
1810
Madrid
Ciudad
Rodrigo
Cuen
21 Aug.
1808
Tagus
27–28 July
1809
Talavera
Toledo
Lisbon
Badajoz
Guadiana
16 May
1811
Medelin
Ciudad Real
1 July 1808:
Capitulation of Dupont's corps
to Spanish troops at Bailen
Cordoba
Bailen
Murc
Guadalquivir
Cartagena
Seville
Granada
Almeria
Málaga
Cádiz
Gibraltar

Iberian Campaigns 1807–14

→ French advance 1807	→ British advance 1808–9	✕ French victory
→ French advance 1808–9	→ British advance 1810–11	✕ British victory
→ French advance 1810–11	→ British advance 1812–14	🏰 fortress

east of Lisbon. The two French commanders were supposed to be co-operating but had no common plans. Marching north, Wellesley surprised Soult at Oporto on 12 May, effectively clearing the French from all but a few fortresses in Portugal. Wellington, as he now may be called after the barony awarded to him following this victory, moved south and in July combined with General Cuesta's 30,000 Spanish troops to advance on Madrid. King Joseph and Marshal Jourdan, his chief of staff, intended to hold this offensive, while ordering three corps from Salamanca to take Wellington in the rear. On 27–28 July Wellington, though his joint forces

PENINSULAR CAMPAIGNS

The Iberian Peninsula was a harsh area with poor resources, and with mountain ranges running from the east to the west. Movement was difficult. Except for one major road, roads were little more than tracks and the terrain difficult. But Napoleon seemed to have forgotten his experience there, a misconception that added to his commanders' problems.

outnumbered the 47,000 French, fought a defensive battle at Talavera, 94 kilometres south-west of Madrid. After repelling determined attacks for two days he was informed by Spanish scouts of the threat to his rear and fell back to Lisbon.

Although at best a tactical success, at home Talavera was celebrated as a victory. The battle did little for British–Spanish military relations. Wellington was convinced that the Spanish forces had let him down, and that their promises of support or supply could not be trusted. Angered, he announced that in future he would not co-operate with Spanish armies unless given full operational command. Meanwhile, in October 1809 British engineers and Portuguese labour began work on the immensely strong series of fortifications – the Lines of Torres Vedras – running 48 kilometres from north of Lisbon to the Tagus estuary. During the winter of 1809–10 the Lisbon area became a secure, almost impregnable stronghold against the expected French invasion of Portugal, and a base for an eventual offensive into Spain.

With Wellington out of the way, the French had no difficulty routing Spanish armies at Ocaña on 19 November and Alba de Tormes on 28 November. In January 1810 Joseph and marshals Soult and Victor, for once acting in concert, launched an offensive into Andalusia and, save for Cádiz, occupied the entire south of the country. Wellington could do little to help. His primary mission was the defence of Portugal, and if the campaign at best had reached a stalemate neither Wellington nor the Spanish commanders were to blame. The blame belonged to the British government that lacked the will to raise an army of a size that a medium continental power could have mustered.

By contrast, after Wagram Napoleon sent massive reinforcements, bringing strength up to 340,000 by August 1810. However, he negated this numerical superiority by decentralizing military authority in Spain, forming the various corps into regional armies – Portugal, Aragón, Catalonia, the North and Centre – taking their orders directly from the emperor. The greater part of this force was tied down to contain pockets of resistance, protect communications, hunt guerrilla bands and besiege Cádiz, leaving but 63,000 to drive the British out of Portugal, the most important strategic task entrusted to Massena.

Geography made Portugal easy to defend against invasion from the east. Most of the Iberian Peninsula was a rugged, barren plateau with major mountain ranges running east to west and the rivers conforming to this pattern. As for Portugal, there were only two practical invasion routes. The fortresses of Ciudad Rodrigo on the Spanish side and Almeida on the Portuguese covered the northern passage, while Badajoz in Spain and Elvas in Portugal guarded the southern approaches. Wellington could muster 30,000 British troops, another 30,000 Portuguese regulars and perhaps 30,000 militia. Yet, with many politicians in London favouring withdrawal from the Peninsula, he adopted a cautious defensive strategy. When, after taking Ciudad Rodrigo in June and Almeida in August, Massena invaded Portugal,

During the winter of 1809–10 British engineers and Portuguese labour built the Lines of Torres Vedras north of Lisbon, stretching from the Tagus river to the Atlantic. Utilizing the advantages of the terrain, these fortifications, not just field entrenchments but solid all-round defensible works, provided Wellington with a secure base against the expected French invasion of Portugal.

Wellington retreated, but on 27 September gave battle in a prepared position on Bussaco Ridge. After repelling several frontal assaults by superior enemy forces, his position was in danger of being turned and Wellington, applying a scorched earth policy, fell back into the Lines of Torres Vedras. His rearguard entered the Lines on 10 October.

Unable to force the Lines, Massena maintained himself in Portugal until March 1811. Then, his forces weakened by hunger and harried by Portuguese irregulars, having lost 25,000 men, he began a slow retreat. Wellington, aware that even now a combination of French corps could crush his small force, followed slowly. The year was spent fighting over the vital key fortresses between Portugal and Spain still in French hands – Almeida, Ciudad Rodrigo and Badajoz. In fact, Massena's reinforced army turned and advanced, 48,000 strong, to relieve Almeida. Wellington met him with 37,000 at Fuentes de Oñoro on 3–5 May. He managed to halt the French advance but could not prevent the Almeida garrison slipping away. At the same time, to the south, Beresford with Anglo-Portuguese forces supported by Spanish regulars was preparing to invest Badajoz. On 16 May he fought a bloody battle at Albuera against Soult. The 6,500 British infantry engaged suffered over two-thirds killed or wounded, but Soult retreated towards Seville. Displeased with Massena's performance Napoleon recalled him. His replacement was Marshal Marmont. But with fewer reinforcements, little co-operation between the marshals and frequent interference from Paris, where Napoleon continued to have delusions about the real situation in the Peninsula, no solution to the problem of how to destroy the insurgents and expel the British could be found.

Even so, until the end of 1811 the French maintained the upper hand in the Peninsula. Following the May battles, British operations for the rest of the year revolved around efforts to take Badajoz and Ciudad Rodrigo, frustrated each time by the lack of an adequate siege-train, entrenching tools and troops. At the same time the French were making territorial gains. Finally, at the onset of winter, Wellington again retired into Portugal, waiting for an opportunity to resume the offensive. The opportunity came when many French veteran formations were withdrawn for the Russian campaign. Wellington resumed offensive operations in January. On 8 January 1812 he appeared before Ciudad Rodrigo and, as soon as practicable breaches were made on 19 January, he sent his storming parties forward. The assault succeeded, but the aftermath was an orgy of looting, rape and murder, repeated on an even more atrocious scale after the storming of Badajoz – a stronger and better-defended fortress – on 6 April. Both incidents, repeated the next year at San Sebastian, illustrated that when a fortress was stormed the garrison often fared better than the civilians. Despite threats of no quarter, soldiers were usually accorded the honours of war or taken prisoner, while the enraged victors took out their pent-up frustrations on the population.

Wellington repeatedly besieged the important frontier fortress of Badajoz. In his second siege during 1811, he blockaded and then besieged Badajoz from 29 May to 19 June, but was short of engineers and proper siege guns. In the illustration an obsolete Portuguese 24-pounder is dragged into position by an ox team.

WELLINGTON'S OFFENSIVES

Wellington now moved forward into Spain, managing to separate Marmont's Army of Portugal from Soult's Army of the South. From mid June to mid July Wellington and Marmont manoeuvred against each other around Salamanca, but, on receipt of intelligence that the French were about to be reinforced from Madrid, Wellington prepared to withdraw back to Portugal. Marmont seized the opportunity and, with about 50,000 on each side, on 22 July attempted to outflank Wellington and cut his line of retreat. This intended *manoeuvre sur les derrières* overextended the French line, and its left wing was crushed. Salamanca was Wellington's greatest victory thus far, revealing the 'peer', as his army called him, to be a cool-headed, resolute and capable battle captain. It cost the French 14,000 casualties and frightened King Joseph into abandoning his capital. Wellington entered Madrid on 12 August.

Salamanca, however, was no Austerlitz. The French in Spain showed remarkable resilience and, evacuating southern Spain, began to mass their remaining forces against Wellington. Marmont, wounded at Salamanca, was replaced by General Clauzel; Marshal Victor lifted the siege of Cádiz in September to join with Soult and King Joseph's troops. To prevent the developing French concentration and capture an important road junction Wellington marched on Burgos, defended by a garrison

*Inspired by their commander, General Jean Louis Dubreton,
a French garrison defended Burgos from 19 September to
22 October 1812 against Wellington's determined efforts. Although
after exploding several mines the British captured the lower part of
the fortifications, Dubreton and his men hung on doggedly to the
citadel until relief forces forced Wellington to abandon the siege.*

of the Armée du Nord. Staunchly defended, this fortress, invested from 9 September to 18 October, repulsed four major assaults and when strong French relief forces approached, Wellington had to raise the siege. In fact, he evacuated Madrid and, suffering substantial losses, retired to winter quarters around Ciudad Rodrigo.

The British commander's caution was justified. Even if French strength in Spain was being steadily eroded, not only by casualties but also by troop withdrawals including the entire Army of Portugal, there remained 200,000 men, guarding central Spain, Valencia and Aragón. Wellington also received reinforcements, including a siege-train, as well as additional Portuguese units, but this only brought his regular forces to about 75,000. In addition, after Salamanca the Spanish government – the *Cortes* – had named him commander-in-chief of all allied forces, adding 21,000 Spanish regulars to his command. Finally, Wellington undertook to improve the armament and organization of several large guerrilla bands. In June 1813 he was ready for his final offensive.

By then the French were no longer fighting to keep Spain but to protect the French border. On orders from Napoleon Joseph gave up Madrid and retreated northwards, unable to establish a defensive line until he crossed the Ebro. Wellington, however, turned his position and, with a new supply base at Santander, and eventually concentrating 70,000 men, attacked King Joseph's main body, just 50,000 strong, at Vitoria on 21 June. Although poorly deployed, the French fought well for a time, but collapsed after their flank was turned. They routed, leaving behind 143 guns and wagon trains loaded with treasure. News of Vitoria raised allied morale in central Europe and contributed to Austria's decision to join the coalition against Napoleon.

Soult was now given command over the remaining French forces, except for Suchet's Army of Aragón. Assembling a force in France, he tried to regain the initiative by crossing the western Pyrenean passes to relieve San Sebastian and Pamplona which were still in French hands. Wellington rapidly restored the situation. After a sixty-nine-day siege San Sebastian fell on 31 August and Pamplona capitulated late in

October, forcing Soult back behind the Nivelle River. On 10 December Wellington attacked this line and penetrated into France. There followed several small engagements in southern France and the final battle was fought on 10 April 1814 when the British took Toulouse. Wellington had come a long way from the Portuguese beaches.

GUERRILLA WAR: AN ASSESSMENT

The empire of the French was not popular. French domination brought political, administrative and religious reforms, sometimes supported by élite groups, while for the peasantry the changes often overturned cherished institutions, customs and beliefs. Conscription, heavy taxes and pillaging offset any advantages of French rule – direct or indirect. Few armies were as rapacious as the French, whose senior officers, including Napoleon and his marshals, as well as generals, officers and soldiers, regarded looting as one of the compensations of war. Even so, while there were peasant risings in many parts of the French empire, there were only three instances of prolonged major armed rebellions: Calabria in 1806, Portugal and Spain after 1808 and the Tyrol in 1809.

When considering popular resistance it is necessary to draw a distinction between militias and other regulated bodies, and guerrillas. Although almost all states had retained theoretical militia obligations, governments and professional soldiers generally tended to have little confidence in militias, and for military and socio-political reasons there was considerable reluctance to arm the general population. The famous *levée en masse* of 1793 aimed to outflank radical demands for a people's war; the Austrian government repeatedly cancelled plans to arm the peasantry, because, as Archduke Charles expressed it, 'they might rouse the sleeping beast'. The rules of war entitled armed civilians serving in properly constituted bodies to combatant status, although militias usually had little combat value and when dispersed might turn into guerrillas, thus blurring the distinction between the combatant and the non-combatant. Military commanders responded with the maximum possible violence in the repression of civilian resistance, creating a vicious circle.

Mounting a major resistance effort depended upon a number of special circumstances including social and political unrest, terrain in which regular troops might find operations difficult, and a population habituated to the use of arms. Thinking of Spain, Clausewitz was to argue that insurrections benefited from the assistance of disciplined regular detachments. During the Napoleonic period resistance movements did not develop a modern national ideology; they remained xenophobic and parochial in nature, and, despite occasional declarations of loyalty to the native dynasty, this was rarely a major motivation. In the Peninsula the ruling dynasties were discredited; Calabria and the Tyrol were aggrieved by royal policies. In all these regions there was friction between the towns and the rural regions. With a tradition of smuggling and banditry, Calabrians were accustomed to firearms, while militia service provided experience with arms on the Iberian Peninsula. The Tyrolean sharpshooters were proud symbols of a free peasantry and provincial pride. In 1809 the Tyroleans fought under their own flag, continuing after Austria had made peace. Emperor Francis's famous question about their leader Andreas Hofer, 'But is he a patriot for me?', was understandable. Finally, all three insurgencies enjoyed outside military support, but, except for Spain, this was inadequate.

The Calabrian and the Tyrolean rebellions can be dealt with fairly briefly; neither acquired strategic importance and ultimately both were put down. In Calabria the Bourbon rule – restored in 1806 – was widely disliked and there was no popular resistance when they were ousted. Requisitioning and disrespect towards the Catholic Church provoked riots, and the French responded by burning villages and by carrying out mass executions. Reprisal led to counter-reprisal, with the British from Sicily providing arms, money and supply, as well as occasional expeditionary forces. Given the small number of French troops, the vast area of the country and the length of the coastline, the region was soon out of control. Hostile to all authority, the peasants turned on

Bourbon troops in the following year; the revolt became a social war, with leadership often provided by the parish clergy and monastic orders. In 1809 King Murat's conscription efforts intensified the revolt, but, lacking central leadership and with British support diminished, the French could concentrate on hunting down the bands of rebellious peasants. By November 1811 the revolt was over, although endemic brigandage continued.

In the Tyrol, centralizing and anti-clerical measures undertaken during the two decades immediately before the French Revolution had caused unrest. After Austria ceded the Tyrol to Bavaria in 1806 the reforming Bavarian chief minister, Count Montgelas, re-introduced these measures, together with new taxes, conscription and the restructuring of local administration. The war party in Vienna therefore found it easy to foment a conspiracy in the Tyrol. Encouraged by the weakness of the Bavarian garrisons and the support of several thousand Austrian regulars, in May 1809 the country rose. Initially the rebels gained dramatic victories, ambushing enemy columns and seizing control of Innsbruck, the capital. Although Austria made peace after Wagram, withdrawing its troops and halting all covert support,

In March 1809 Tyrolean patriots led by Andreas Hofer rose up against Bavarian rule and, supported by a few Austrian regulars, liberated almost their entire country by the end of May. In the end, of course, French and Bavarian troops re-established control. This patriotic illustration shows the departure of a poorly armed 'last levy'.

the rebels fought on, still winning some victories. In the end, exhaustion, hunger and concentric operations against their strongholds ended the revolt in early 1810.

Austrian sponsors of the revolt had believed that the uprising would find a response in Germany. They were wrong. The Bavarians and Tyroleans hated each other; they gave no quarter and they committed unspeakable atrocities. Moreover, when, despite imperial orders to lay down their arms, the Tyroleans fought on, it confirmed the misgivings held by those in authority about an armed populace in Vienna. In 1813 the Austrian authorities declined to raise popular insurrections.

Finally, there was the most important people's war, Spain and Portugal, so indispensable to eventual British victory that the very word 'guerrilla' – Spanish for small war – entered into the language. The intense resistance to the French defies rational explanation. The Bourbon monarchy was hardly more Spanish than Joseph Bonaparte, while the country suffered under widespread absentee land ownership and clerical abuses, retaining a strong tradition of local and provincial loyalties. King Joseph represented land reform and effective civil administration – changes that were advantageous to most Spaniards – yet the peasantry remained indifferent or even hostile to economic or political reform. Initial resistance had flared up when French columns had entered Spain and Portugal expecting to live off the land. Napoleon had told Junot that 'an army of 20,000 can subsist even in a desert'. Widespread foraging and looting, from a population already living in abject poverty and near starvation, became a principal cause of the bitter resistance. By 1809 this phase had passed, however. The French were in Madrid, and had the Spaniards accepted the Bonapartist regime then most of the foreign soldiers would have departed. Instead, the interference of the French with the royal family had ignited an urban as well as a rural revolt.

In its first stages of the revolt, from 1808 to 1810, towns like Saragossa withstood formal sieges for weeks at a time, with the defenders, soldiers, clerics and civilians continuing to resist from house to house after their fortifications had been breached. The mass insurgency did not survive. Instead, with the mountainous and almost roadless terrain providing ideal conditions for guerrilla operations, armed peasants, often joined by soldiers, coalesced into permanent bands, some operating under government authority, some self-constituted, and some degenerating into outright banditry. Waging a small war of ambushes, raids and attacks against soft targets, the bands maintained themselves by captured supplies and by extorting food, clothing and 'taxes' from the peasantry. Few of the Spanish or Portuguese irregulars spared the wounded or prisoners, women or children. Bestial murder and torture were common, the French retaliating in like manner. Until early 1812 the French were able to contain the guerrillas and even recapture previously lost territory, but the presence of Wellington's army, and that of a smaller force based on Cádiz, prevented them from concentrating against the bands.

Of Napoleon's commanders, only Marshal Suchet, commanding in Aragón, succeeded in meeting the challenge of the insurgency. He combined effective military action with political and social reforms and he sternly suppressed all looting. Only in Aragón were French soldiers able to move about singly and unarmed, while villagers took up arms against the guerrillas. However, such pacification was clearly an exception. As the years passed some of the guerrilla bands assumed a more regular character. Leaders such as Espoz y Mina, in almost total control of Navarre, and Don Julian Sanchez in León, received government commissions and co-operated closely with the British; in the region outside Madrid El Empecinado commanded 2,000 foot and 500 horse. Even so, the bands could not liberate Spain or secure areas against French retaliation. Had it not been for Wellington's army, they would ultimately have been defeated. The liberation of Spain was the result of Wellington's victory, one to which they had contributed much.

By that time, of course, Napoleon had suffered a far more decisive defeat in Russia, a defeat that had shaken the very foundations of his empire.

CHAPTER SIX

Russia, Germany and France 1812–14

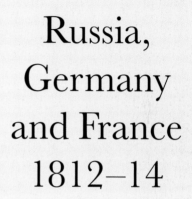

After rallying to break through the Russian Army and establishing bridgeheads on the western bank of the Beresina, French engineers constructed two trestle bridges; fighting off greatly superior numbers of pursuing Russians, between 26 and 29 November 1812 some 40,000 combatants and thousands of stragglers managed to get across.

Russia, Germany and France

THE INVASION OF RUSSIA was not unexpected. Relations had deteriorated since Tilsit. At best a reluctant ally in 1809, Tsar Alexander had become apprehensive about Napoleon's ultimate intentions in Poland, the Balkans and Germany, while the Continental System damaged Russia's economy. In late December 1810 he ended compliance with the system, approached Sweden for an alliance and looked to make peace with the Ottoman Empire. Napoleon, who could not tolerate Russia openly defying agreements, suspected her of designs on the Grand Duchy of Warsaw and of secret ambitions towards the Ottoman Empire. By 1811 both sides were preparing for war, though it was Napoleon and not Alexander who initiated hostilities.

THE OPPOSING ARMIES AND WAR PLANS

Since 1808 the Russian Army had been modernized by Alexei Arakcheev, Minister of War from 1808 to 1810, and Barclay de Tolly, his successor. Although a brutal reactionary, Arakcheev was a good artillerist who introduced a new range of weapons: the System of 1805 comprised of 6- and 12-pounder cannons and 10- and 20-pounder howitzers with screw-elevating mechanisms and improved sights. By 1812 there were some 1,699 guns and a doctrine stressing massed fire. Barclay undertook infantry reform. An unusual officer, having served fourteen years in the ranks, he tried to improve the soldiers' conditions, reducing emphasis on drill and stressing marksmanship, though commanders continued to favour columns and the bayonet over the firefight. Administratively, Barclay reduced the large clumsy infantry divisions to contain three brigades, divisional cavalry and artillery. Finally, just before the French invasion, he introduced corps, each of two infantry divisions, cavalry and artillery, in the First and Second Western armies.

Rivalries and intrigues within the high command, divided between the 'German' and 'Russian' factions, impeded reforms. Among the most influential members of the German faction was the elderly

General von Phull, a Prussian who in good eighteenth-century fashion believed that the conduct of war was a science. Barclay, a Livonian of Scots descent, also belonged to the 'German' faction, while the Russian group was headed by the 67-year-old Kutuzov. A charismatic leader, he had little patience with the modern ways introduced by Barclay, whom he replaced early in the 1812 campaign.

When war appeared imminent the tsar made peace with Sweden and the Turks, releasing troops from these fronts. On paper the Russian Army numbered 600,000, but could only field the two western armies immediately, about 220,000 men. The war plan, conceived by Phull, exploited strategic depth. Barclay's First Army, about 127,000 strong, was to withdraw to the entrenched camp at Drissa on the Dvina river. Meanwhile, Bagration's 48,000-strong Second Army, posted north of the Pripet Marshes, would move to attack the right flank of the invaders. A third army was assembling far to the south, and troops from Moldavia and Finland marched to join the western armies.

Napoleon was well aware of the difficulties ahead. In addition to careful study of the history and geography of Russia, his 1807 campaign in Poland had provided experience fighting in an underpopulated area with poor to non-existent roads and extreme weather conditions. Therefore he made extensive logistic preparations. Enormous quantities of supply were amassed in depots behind the front, and to bring supplies forward he assembled a vast supply train – 25,000 vehicles, not counting ammunition caissons, forges and ambulances. Some of the transport companies received draft oxen, but, even so, the train required 90,000 horses, the artillery 30,000 and the cavalry over 80,000. The supply wagons could lift 7,000 tonnes daily, but beyond a certain point the draught animals would consume their payload. Lift capacity clearly was inadequate to provide fodder for the horses, but Napoleon expected that by June new grass would provide pasture. The arrangements might have sufficed had Napoleon succeeded in destroying the Russian armies in a short, decisive campaign near the frontier.

THE INVASION OF RUSSIA, 1812

There were several major problems facing this campaign. Perhaps most serious was the question of supply. Although nine large depots had been laid down from Königsberg to Warsaw, available transport could not keep up with the pace of advance. Second, the huge size of the army and its wide frontage required the creation of new command structures, de facto army groups. Given the technical limitations of the era, neither problem could be solved.

1 May 1812: Napoleon leaves Paris with parts of French contingent to form the Grande Armeé de la Russie

DENMARK

Copen

Hamburg
Bremen
Hanover
Amsterdam
Cologne
Wesar
CONFEDERATION
Nuremberg
OF THE
RHINE
Strasbourg · Stuttgart · Munich
Metz
Reims
Salzburg
Innsbruck
Zurich
HELVETIA
Berne · Geneva
KINGDOM
Verona · Trieste
Milan
Turin
Genoa
Bologna
Florence
ITALY
Rome
KINGD
Naples
NAP

UNITED KINGDOM
Dublin · London
Bristol
Thames
Severn

Rouen · Paris
Orléans
Tours
Nantes
Limoges · Clermont-Ferrand
FRENCH EMPIRE
Lyons
Loire
Saône

ATLANTIC OCEAN

Bordeaux
Garonne · Dordogne
Toulouse

Nice
Marseille

CORSICA

Barcelona

SPAIN

SARDINIA

Caligari

Mediterranean Sea

PALERMO · Messina
SICILY · Catania

Tunis

6 Garrison, depot and other second line troops left to guard France's Spanish territories

Algiers

OTTOMAN EMPIRE

ALGERIA

May 1812: concentration areas of **2** central Germany, approximately 614,000 men, 200,000 animals (including cavalry mounts and food on the hoof) and 25,000 vehicles

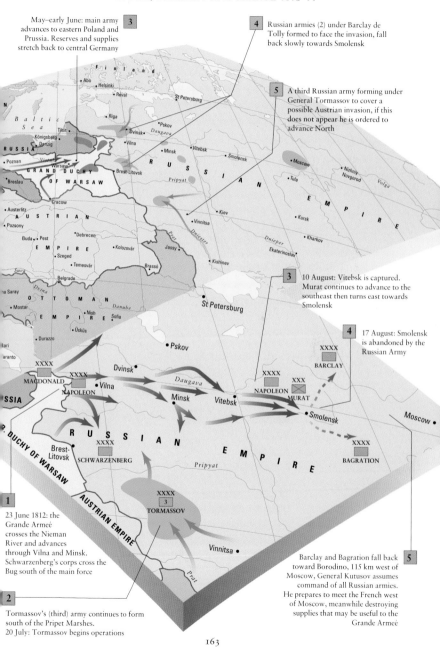

3 May–early June: main army advances to eastern Poland and Prussia. Reserves and supplies stretch back to central Germany

4 Russian armies (2) under Barclay de Tolly formed to face the invasion, fall back slowly towards Smolensk

5 A third Russian army forming under General Tormassov to cover a possible Austrian invasion, if this does not appear he is ordered to advance North

3 10 August: Vitebsk is captured. Murat continues to advance to the southeast then turns east towards Smolensk

4 17 August: Smolensk is abandoned by the Russian Army

1 23 June 1812: the Grande Armée crosses the Nieman River and advances through Vilna and Minsk. Schwarzenberg's corps cross the Bug south of the main force

2 Tormassov's (third) army continues to form south of the Pripet Marshes. 20 July: Tormassov begins operations

5 Barclay and Bagration fall back toward Borodino, 115 km west of Moscow, General Kutusov assumes command of all Russian armies. He prepares to meet the French west of Moscow, meanwhile destroying supplies that may be useful to the Grande Armée

Napoleon realized that he needed a larger army if he was to overwhelm the tough Russians. By the spring of 1812 he had massed an immense force: 614,000 including reserves and rear area troops, the 'army of twenty nations' as it was called. His first line consisted of 449,000 men of whom fewer than one-third were French, the remainder Dutch, Westphalian, Polish, Bavarian, Saxon, Austrian, Prussian, Croatian, Dalmatian, Swiss, Italian, Portuguese and even Spanish. The size of this army dictated a direct approach along the line of greatest expectations north of the Pripet Marshes, close to his Baltic supply ports and threatening both Moscow and St Petersburg. Such unprecedented numbers and the width of their deployment, about 480 kilometres, posed command problems. Napoleon had introduced a new formation – the army group – but with long-distance communications depending on mounted messengers he was unable to command and control armies effectively over such vast distances. And his senior subordinates were poorly prepared for independent command.

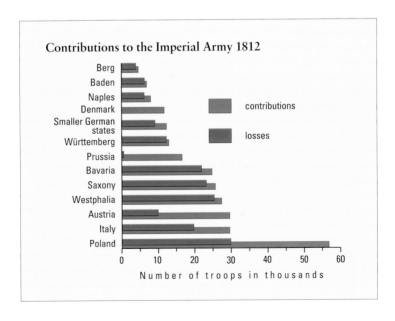

Contributions to the Imperial Army 1812

The march on Moscow

On 4 June 1812 the Grande Armée crossed the Niemen into Russia. The central column consisted of three armies, commanded by Napoleon, Eugène and Jerome respectively, echeloned back to Warsaw. On his distant flanks were two semi-autonomous formations. On his left was Macdonald's corps, including a Prussian auxiliary contingent and two Bavarian divisions; on his extreme right was the Austrian auxiliary corps commanded by Prince Schwarzenberg. Additional formations were in reserve and along the line of communications.

Napoleon's plan was for his main force – three infantry and two cavalry corps, the Imperial Guard now 47,000 strong, supported by Eugène's Army of Italy – to destroy Barclay's army in a series of envelopments. Jerome was to lure Bagration towards Warsaw, stalling him at the Narew or Bug river line until, having disposed of Barclay, Napoleon would sweep into his rear. The plan looked grand on paper, but failed partly because the enemy was able to evade battle, but above all because of supply and command problems. Napoleon's deteriorating health delayed operational decisions. Often lethargic, he could not handle so large an army on so wide a front, while his principal subordinates, when faced with operational or even strategic decisions, failed to exploit opportunities.

The Russian retreat continued. Attempts to envelop Barclay around Vilna failed when Eugène was late in moving up on the right flank. Vilna was occupied without a fight on 26 June. Here Napoleon tarried for three weeks, while, led by Murat's troopers, his main force followed Barclay towards Vitebsk. The army had begun its march in suffocating heat, followed after 29 June by five days of pouring rain. The dirt roads turned to seas of mud, impassable for supply trains and artillery. With few rations coming through, men suffered from hunger and fatigue, and though many villages had not been burnt – the scorched earth policy was a later myth – the pace set by Murat's cavalry did not permit foraging. The army halted from 29 July to 12 August at Vitebsk to rest the troops and allow artillery and supply columns to catch up.

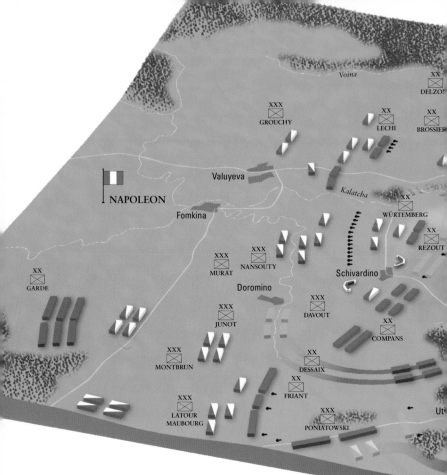

Voina

XX
DELZO?

XXX
GROUCHY

XX
LECHI

XX
BROSSIER

Valuyeva

Kalatcha

NAPOLEON

XX
WÜRTEMBERG

Fomkina

XX
REZOUT

XXX
MURAT

XXX
NANSOUTY

Schivardino

XX
GARDE

Doromino

XXX
JUNOT

XXX
DAVOUT

XX
COMPANS

XXX
MONTBRUN

XX
DESSAIX

XX
FRIANT

XXX
LATOUR
MAUBOURG

XXX
PONIATOWSKI

Ut?

Napoleon had penetrated deep into
Russia, but without fighting a major battle; his army
had lost close to one-third of its strength in men and horses from
exhaustion and disease.

Meantime Jerome had failed to engage Bagration. On 1 July the
impatient emperor dispatched Davout to move south from Vilna to
intercept the Second Army and trap the Russians between the two
French forces. There was a communications' slip-up between Davout
and Jerome. When Jerome discovered he had been subordinated to
Davout he quit his command and returned to Westphalia. Bagration,
meanwhile, escaped north. Directed to prevent a link-up of the Russian

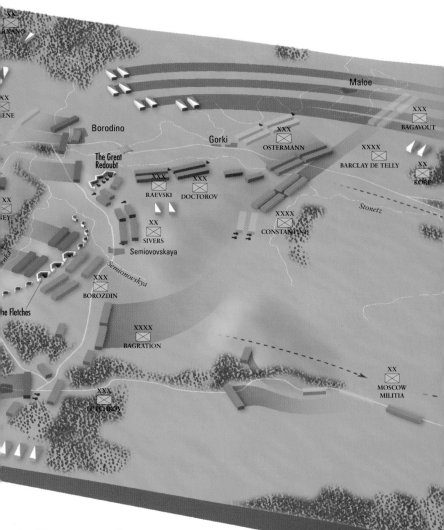

Maloe

XXX BAGAVOUT

XXX OSTERMANN

XXXX BARCLAY DE TELLY

XX KORF

Borodino

Gorki

The Great Redoubt

XXX RAEVSKI

XXX DOCTOROV

Stonetz

XXXX CONSTANTINE

XX SIVERS

Semiovovskaya

Semionovskaya

XXX BOROZDIN

he Fletches

XXXX BAGRATION

XX MOSCOW MILITIA

XXX TUTCHKOV

THE BATTLE OF BORODINO

*On 7 September 1812 Napoleon had an opportunity to
destroy the Russian Army. Although Davout proposed to turn the Russian left,
the emperor insisted on a series of frontal attacks against the Russians deployed
behind extensive earthworks. When at last the Great Redoubt in the Russian centre
was taken by a massive cavalry charge he refused to use his reserve, the Imperial
Guard, to exploit it and the Russians withdrew to survive as an army.*

armies, Davout followed Bagration but failed to bring the Russians to battle. To the north Napoleon compelled Barclay to abandon his entrenched camp and positions along the Dvina. The two Russian armies managed to link up on 4 August, falling back on Smolensk, a city on the Dniepr halfway between the Niemen and Moscow. Barclay, pressured by Alexander, Bagration and his own staff, fought an indecisive three-day battle, 17–19 August, but then evacuated the city. Although bitterly assailed for this decision, he had no choice. Napoleon had crossed the river further east, turning his position. Even so, because General Junot failed to cut the Smolensk–Moscow road as ordered, the Russians managed an orderly retreat.

Smolensk had cost Napoleon 10,000 casualties. With troops left in garrisons, with Oudinot and St Cyr detached to help Macdonald in the north and General Reynier sent south to assist Schwarzenberg, Napoleon's main force was reduced to about 130,000 men. But its heaviest losses continued to be due to administrative and logistic breakdowns: vast amounts of stores were dumped for want of transport; medical supplies were totally inadequate; dysentery and

typhus, aggravated by near starvation, decimated the army. Napoleon faced a critical decision. Should he consolidate his position and renew his offensive in 1813, or should he press on? Moscow lay 448 kilometres to the east and the emperor was convinced that the Russians would fight a decisive battle to defend their capital. On 28 August the army resumed its advance, Murat leading and Davout trying to keep up.

On the Russian side Kutuzov, now a prince and a field marshal, had replaced Barclay, widely denounced for his attrition strategy. He intended to fight at the crossroad village of Borodino, 105 kilometres west of Moscow. On 7 September an obviously sick Napoleon, disregarding Davout's advice for turning the Russian left, insisted on sending repeated infantry column attacks against heavily gunned field fortifications. The Russians counter-attacked in compact masses. After

On 7 September 1812 Kutuzov decided to stand and, his front protected by extensive field works, confront the Grande Armée. The battle, one of the few frontal battles fought by Napoleon, was only a qualified victory, clearing the road to Moscow. But the Russian Army survived.

battering each other without clear result, at about 4 p.m. a desperate French infantry-cavalry assault captured the Great Redoubt in the centre of the Russian position. Exploitation by reserves could have destroyed the Russian Army. Napoleon still had 30,000 Imperial Guard infantry but would not commit them. 'I will not have my Guard destroyed. When you have come 800 leagues from France you do not wreck your last reserve.' At the cost of more than 30,000 casualties the road to Moscow was open, but during the night Kutuzov, with about 90,000 combat capable troops remaining, slipped away towards Kaluga south-east of Moscow. On 14 September, with 95,000 men, Napoleon entered the near-deserted city.

THE RETREAT FROM MOSCOW

Napoleon had come 885 kilometres from his start line but failed to destroy the Russian Army or the will to resist. His strategic system, which depended on mass and mobility to smash the enemy early in a campaign and bring him to terms, failed against the Russians, who bartered space to compensate for numerical and tactical inferiority. At the end of a vulnerable supply line, Napoleon could not afford to stay in partially burnt Moscow; on 19 October, he began his retreat. Initially he intended to follow a southerly route through the Kaluga district, still well supplied with food and fodder. Kutuzov tried to intercept at Maloyaroslavets, and though the battle was indecisive it induced Napoleon to return to the northern route via Borodino to Smolensk.

Lack of discipline as much as the winter destroyed his army. Over 40,000 vehicles of all kinds, loaded with loot instead of supplies, accompanied the army, slowing down its progress, wasting remaining horses. When the first heavy snow fell on 4 November restraint collapsed. Guns and wagons were abandoned; thousands of starving men left their units to forage and were killed by Cossacks or peasants. The column began to stretch out and it took four days, 9–14 November, for the 50,000-strong remnant to reach Smolensk where any remaining discipline vanished. Pillage, drunkenness and murder were common,

French advance troops under Murat are entering Moscow on 14 September 1814. The picture is fanciful: the French entered around midnight and the city had been largely evacuated on the orders of its Russian governor.

looters destroying vital supplies. Napoleon had hoped to halt at Smolensk, but this had clearly become impossible. Retreat now turned into rout, only the Guard and the rearguard led by the indomitable Ney, musket in hand, retaining some semblance of order.

And yet there would be occasions when the retreating hordes behaved like an army and the emperor, awaking from his stupor, like a great commander. While the flank corps fell back on the main body, adding some combat capability, Kutuzov shadowed the retreating column and on 17 November, with 90,000 men, tried to intercept it at Krasnoi, 40 kilometres south-west of Smolensk. A determined attack by the Guard convinced Kutuzov to seek no further engagement until he combined with Wittgenstein and Tshitshagov's Army of Moldavia. The combined armies, 144,000 strong, converged against Napoleon's 37,000 exhausted soldiers, who were followed by vast numbers of stragglers. On 22 November the Army of Moldavia captured the crucial depots at Minsk, and moved on to seize the only bridge crossing the broad Beresina river, completing encirclement of the

French. To make matters worse, an unseasonable thaw had turned the frozen river into a raging torrent.

At this point Napoleon regained some of his old fire. He ordered Oudinot, commanding the lead corps, to retrieve the bridge. Against all odds the marshal almost succeeded, but, having failed, managed to engage the Russians for four days until the main army closed up. On 26 November Oudinot demonstrated against the Russians at Borizov. By then a possible crossing point had been located some 18 kilometres upstream at Studienka. While Oudinot diverted Russian attention, some 400 heroic French engineers, working in the freezing water, built two wooden bridges. Oudinot's corps crossed first, Ney, Victor,

After Napoleon left for France on 5 December 1812, Murat was unable to give direction to the army while the remaining marshals did little to rally the remaining troops. Only Ney came out of the disaster with an enhanced reputation, commanding, musket in hand, the rearguard against the pursuing Cossacks.

Junot, Davout and Murat followed. Fierce fighting around the eastern and the western bridgeheads continued until the morning of 29 November, when French engineers destroyed the bridges. In the last minutes mobs of stragglers rushed the bridges. Some 35,000 French survivors escaped the trap, leaving behind about 50,000 dead or captured, including non-combatants. Napoleon and the marshals had done the impossible – if, during a bitter retreat, the crossing of the Beresina still was a victory.

Now winter descended in earnest. The cold again became so intense that both French and Russians lost fighting capabilities, though Cossacks continued to harry Ney's rearguard. Napoleon left on 5 December, returning to Paris to start raising new armies for the coming year. In terrible weather, with Murat left in command, the survivors staggered on, walking skeletons in rags. On 8 December they reached Vilna where there were 4 million rations in the depots, but with discipline totally gone the depots were looted. Moreover, Murat feared being caught by the Russians, who were in fact far behind and content to have the weather destroy the French. Abandoning his rear units, he marched on to Kovno and from there into Poland and East Prussia, from where he bolted for Naples, leaving Eugène to conduct the final stages of the retreat. On 14 December the last French soldier, Marshal Ney, crossed the last bridge over the Niemen.

Napoleon would campaign again and campaign well, but it was only a matter of time before his enemies would unite against him and, provided they remained united, would prevail by sheer weight of numbers.

Prussian military reforms

Even before the year was out Prussia left her French alignment. On 30 December 1812 General von Yorck, a conservative officer but a progressive tactician who had handled his corps to avoid major engagements, signed the Convention of Tauroggen, breaking the French connection and compelling his reluctant king to act. Fleeing Berlin and its French garrison Frederick William escaped to Silesia, mobilized his army, called for volunteers and introduced conscription. On 28 February 1813 Prussia signed a military convention with Russia. To the south Vienna had instructed Schwarzenberg, whose corps had suffered 7,000 killed in action and 4,000 dead of disease, to extricate his troops. On 30 January 1813 he signed a convention neutralizing his corps, and retreated into Galicia. Technically, Austria remained Napoleon's ally; in reality, however, Vienna, where Chancellor Metternich now dominated affairs, adopted a policy of armed neutrality waiting to join the winning side.

The wars of 1813–14 are known in German history as the Wars of Liberation, but dislike of the French rather than German nationalism and liberal aspirations was the driving force. Napoleon's overthrow was not the result of popular movements, but of the combined efforts of the great powers, all basically conservative. Even Prussian mobilization was not as uniformly enthusiastic as later nationalist legend made out. The king and the nobility had misgivings about popular aspects of recent military reforms; the peasants were aware that they would have to pay most of the cost in blood. But Prussia was committed. The Russians entered Berlin on 4 March 1813, and war against France was declared on 17 March, the king summoning all his subjects – 'Brandenburgers, Prussians, Silesians, Pomeranians, Lithuanians' – to fight. It was a conservative proclamation, not an appeal for a national insurrection.

Even so, the Prussian Army of 1813 differed in important ways from that of 1806. The débâcle of 1806 demanded a drastic overhaul of Prussian society and the army. The Treaty of Tilsit and the Convention of Paris had deprived Prussia of her richest provinces and almost half of her population. Her only hope for regaining her former political and military position lay in harnessing all remaining resources: political, economic and military reform had to proceed hand-in-hand with reform of the body politic. The leaders of the political and military reform factions agreed to abolish feudal benefits and serfdom, and on making military service universal – not a burden but a citizen's proud privilege. Conservative opposition and French intervention prevented the full implementation of these reforms. None the less, the efforts of the military reform faction, led by Major General von Scharnhorst, ensured that in 1813 new commanders, staff procedures and combat doctrine guided the Prussian Army.

Immediately, the forced reduction of the army to 42,000 men enabled the reformers to purge the officer corps. By 1809, out of the 142 generals of 1806, 17 had been cashiered, 86 honourably dismissed and only 22 retained on active duty, with similar reductions in the lesser grades. Although new regulations opened entry into the commissioned ranks to all citizens with the required educational and moral qualifications, in practice the aristocratic element continued to dominate the officer corps.

Reorganization created mixed brigades instead of divisions, but the most important innovation was a new general staff concept. The reformers hoped that the collective intelligence of highly trained staff officers would offset individual genius, and in 1810 opened a new school, later the War Academy, to instruct promising officers. In contrast to other armies where the chief of staff only implemented his commander's orders, the Prussian system envisaged the chief of staff as a full partner in command decisions. In 1813 the most famous of these command teams was that of Blücher and von Gneisenau.

Manpower, equipment and weapons remained difficult problems. Restricted to 42,000 men, attempts to increase numbers by enrolling supernumeraries yielded little. Counting reserves the army numbered 52,523 in 1807 and only 65,675 when war was declared in 1813. War forced the king to enlarge his forces by calling for volunteer *Jäger* detachments and establishing a militia, the *Landwehr*. The *Jäger*, only 12,000 strong, were recruited from young men able to pay for their equipment and uniforms; their military contribution was limited. As for the *Landwehr*, its strength set at 120,000 – volunteers if possible, but conscripted if necessary – military effectiveness varied. Recruited mainly from the poor, many units lacked weapons, clothing and equipment. Their morale initially was shaky and was certainly not improved by harsh discipline. Some units fought with great courage, others collapsed at the first encounter with the enemy. But they learned to fight by fighting, and by autumn differences in combat performance with the line had become small, and massive deliveries of British arms, equipment, and clothing had overcome shortages. Having reached its projected strength, the *Landwehr* was integrated into the field army, and then formed into four army corps and the Guard.

THE RECOVERY OF THE FRENCH ARMY

Raising a new army for the 1813 campaign was one of Napoleon's greatest administrative achievements. His ultimate goal was 700,000 men, including the 200,000 still fighting in Spain. In October 1812 he had sent cadres for new regiments back from Moscow to France where the conscripts of 1813 were already training. These, together with recalled veterans, 16,000 men from Spain, embodied units of the National Guard, drafts of sailors and naval gunners, made up a force of over 120,000 men, supplemented by the 1814 conscripts called in February 1813. Loyal for the moment despite the losses incurred in Russia, the Confederation of the Rhine began to rebuild its forces, and Prince Poniatowski and 10,000 faithful Poles were ready for action. In April the emperor moved east to join the 50,000 troops under Eugène still holding the fortresses of the Saale and Elbe rivers. By the middle of the month he had assembled 226,000 men and 457 guns, with 120,000 men under his personal command. The build-up completed in August, Napoleon had over 400,000 men, including 88,000 in foreign contingents.

The quality of this vast mass was indifferent. The French infantry, young and inexperienced, was enthusiastic, but lacked training and stamina; the cavalry was inferior to that lost in Russia, its mounts poor and its troopers inexperienced. Deficiencies in cavalry and uninspired leadership – even the marshals were tired of war – gravely affected operational efficiency. But his opponents were still weak in numbers, perhaps 110,000 Russians and Prussians. Kutuzov was nominated supreme commander but died in April, and Tsar Alexander I, as ever convinced of his military talents, arrived in Germany. For the time being, the Prussians were mainly under Blücher, the Russians under Wittgenstein.

Napoleon had envisaged a rapid sweep through Prussia to relieve besieged Danzig, but modified this plan. While forces under Eugène moved to link up, Napoleon's Army of the Main entered Saxony and on 2 May defeated the Prusso-Russians at Grossgörschen. Lacking adequate reconnaissance capability, Ney and Marmont, 45,000 strong initially, faced 75,000, but Napoleon had reinforced his numbers to 110,000 by late afternoon and steadied Ney's wavering divisions. At about 6 p.m., with Tsar Alexander hesitating to commit his Guard, Napoleon established a grand battery of seventy guns to pound the enemy, then sent the Young Guard followed by the Old Guard into the breach. The enemy collapsed. Again Napoleon had demonstrated his ability to pin superior numbers, reinforce the decisive point and counter-attack. His weakness in cavalry, a major factor in the allied decision to attack, prevented all-out pursuit and the enemy retired in good order towards Dresden.

Napoleon, having rapidly combined his forces into one army, advanced on Bautzen, 52 kilometres north-east of Dresden, where Wittgenstein, reinforced to 96,000 men and 450 guns, had taken up a strong position. Napoleon followed with 115,000 and 150 guns, detaching Ney with 85,000 to demonstrate towards Berlin, hoping to draw the Prussians north to defend their capital. Failing this, Napoleon intended to pin the enemy by a frontal attack on 20 May, while the next day Ney would execute a *manoeuvre sur les derrières* to deliver the decisive blow. Then, and later, Ney lacked the skill needed to handle a major independent command. On 21 May he committed tactical blunders that allowed the Allies to escape, the French again unable to pursue effectively. Napoleon's plan had been excellent but the execution flawed. With some 20,000 casualties on each side the results were inconclusive.

Wittgenstein, blamed for the setback, actually the fault of Alexander's amateurish interference, resigned command and was replaced by Barclay, who believed that the Allies would have to fall back into Poland, an option Blücher and Gneisenau opposed. In the end they agreed to retreat to positions south-west of Berlin, shielding the capital and Silesia. Napoleon entered Dresden; Davout occupied Hamburg. At this point both sides needed a rest and, on 4 June, Napoleon accepted an allied armistice proposal, eventually extended until 17 August. During this period diplomatic negotiations continued, but had little substance. Both sides reorganized and reinforced, but the Allies had more to gain than Napoleon. With England a generous paymaster, more states joined the Allies. On 3 March Bernadotte, since 1810 Crown Prince and effective ruler of Sweden, formerly a marshal conspicuous for his absence from battles, concluded an alliance with Britain. Two months later advance elements of his army landed in Pomerania. The Swedish troops were welcome, but the decisive event was Austria's accession to the coalition.

In Vienna Napoleon's Russian disaster created pressure for immediate war, but Metternich had no intention of unleashing popular emotions, fearing that premature action would only result in replacing French with Russian hegemony in Germany. He maintained the guise of neutrality, negotiating with both sides while authorizing covert, later overt, mobilization. By the end of May an Austrian army under Schwarzenberg, with Major General Radetzky as his chief of staff, had assembled. On 14 June Metternich authorized full mobilization, calling up reservists and the *Landwehr*. Despite severe shortages in arms and equipment, by August a very considerable army, almost 200,000 men, was concentrated in Bohemia. In addition, the Army of Inner Austria mustered about 37,000 and there were another 39,000 along the Danube. Making further efforts, by the end of August, Austria had 479,000 men under arms, with 298,000 combatants.

On 26 June Metternich met with Napoleon and delivered unacceptable terms. When, as expected, these were rejected, Austria joined Prussia, Russia and Sweden the following day. In round numbers the coalition had 800,000 against Napoleon's 600,000, which, excluding minor theatres of operations, garrisons and rear echelons, came to

570,000 against 410,000. With Austria providing the largest contingent, Metternich insisted on naming the supreme commander. His choice was Schwarzenberg, not because of his military talents but because his aristocratic background and diplomatic experience were ideal for coping with the problems of coalition warfare, made even more difficult because of the presence of three sovereigns at headquarters.

THE 1813 AUTUMN CAMPAIGN

When fighting resumed on 14 August after Blücher had violated the armistice, Schwarzenberg managed to get the Allies to adopt a common strategy, the so-called Trachenberg Plan. Its basic idea was for whichever of the allied armies faced the emperor in person to refuse battle, while the others closed in. In general, this scheme was followed during the six weeks of indecisive fighting. Napoleon planned to divide the Allies by an advance on Berlin, while he contained the Austrians in Saxony. Oudinot was given 120,000 men including Davout's 35,000 at Hamburg, to threaten Berlin and defeat the Prussians and Swedes, Ney was given 85,000, and Napoleon commanded the largest army – 165,000. In practice Napoleon also commanded Ney's force and drew on Oudinot when needed. Choosing Oudinot over Davout to command his second strongest army, away from the main force, was poor judgement. Davout, with proven ability for independent command, was far more suitable, but Napoleon left him in a near static role east of Hamburg. If Davout rather than Oudinot had commanded against Bernadotte, the outcome of the autumn campaign might have been different.

Oudinot won the early encounters, unnerving Bernadotte who proposed to evacuate Berlin. General von Bülow, his chief Prussian subordinate, refused and on 23 August, at Grossbeeren, 14 kilometres south of Berlin, threw back one of Oudinot's corps. Oudinot retreated, compelling Davout, who had advanced eastwards, to fall back to Hamburg. Meanwhile, leaving 20,000 under St Cyr to hold Dresden, Napoleon had turned against Blücher's Army of Silesia. Complying with the Trachenberg Plan, Blücher retired,

while Schwarzenberg attacked Dresden. Receiving requests for urgent help, Napoleon reversed his army, assigning Macdonald to contain Blücher. With his young conscripts showing that they could not only fight but could also march, he arrived back in Dresden by 26 August. The next day 120,000 against 150,000 defeated Schwarzenberg, but again could not pursue effectively. Vandamme's corps,

1. April: Napoleon concentrates his army to face Allied forces

2. May: driving the Allied forces eastwards, Napoleon is victorious at Lützen and Dresden

3. 4 June–16 August: armistice, Napoleon uses the time to train his inexperienced army

4. 12 August: Austria declares war

5. 26–27 August: battle of Dresden

6. September–October: after suffering defeats, ending with the battle of Leipzig, the French army withdraws to the Rhine

7. 30–31 October: Bavarian-Austrian army attacks the retreating French but is beaten off

THE CAMPAIGN IN GERMANY, APRIL–JUNE 1813

With his army rebuilt and a number of fortresses in eastern Germany still held, Napoleon took up a central position in Saxony and from there tried to make separate thrusts against the Prusso-Russian armies, hoping that a major victory would lead them to abandon the war. These fail, but by June both sides are exhausted and agree on an armistice. When hostilities resume Napoleon concentrates at Leipzig.

sent to block the Austrian retreat, was isolated and destroyed at Kulm on the 29th. In the east Blücher had turned against Macdonald and on the 26th mauled him at the Katzbach. As for the Berlin front, where Ney superseded Oudinot in command, Ney again demonstrated his incapacity for independent command. On 6 September 50,000 Prussians defeated Ney at Dennewitz, 60 kilometres south-west of the Prussian capital, nullifying the effects of Napoleon's victory at Dresden.

For the rest of the month Napoleon moved alternately against each of his foes, but could not bring them to battle. His German allies were wavering; Bavaria defected on 8 October. He had retired behind the Elbe on 24 September and on 12 October marched to make a stand at Leipzig. His strategic situation was bad, three allied armies were closing in, but Napoleon still hoped to defeat them in detail. The 'Battle of the Nations', 16–19 October, was a series of bloody actions, ultimately pitting 335,000 allied troops against 190,000 French. Schwarzenberg came into action first. He might have been defeated on the 15th, but Napoleon waited for Ney's arrival. And with that the Austrians almost were beaten on the 16th, but saved by Blücher's arrival. There was little action the following day, but on 18 October strong Russian reinforcements arrived and Bernadotte's army finally came into line. Early on 19 October, undefeated but fearing encirclement, Napoleon began a

THE BATTLE OF THE NATIONS: LEIPZIG 16–19 OCTOBER 1813

The largest battle of the Napoleonic Wars consisted of a series of bloody engagements around the city of Leipzig during which Napoleon, fighting against great odds, failed to beat the converging Allies. Allied attacks also failed, but as pressure grew and his Saxon troops defected, he withdrew across the Elster river. During the retreat Napoleon defeated a Bavarian attempt to intercept him at Hanau on 30–31 October and reached France with some 70,000 men in formed units and another 40,000 stragglers.

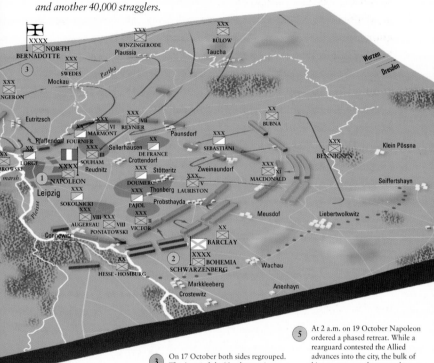

1 The battle was fought for three days around and in the town of Leipzig. Counting in reinforcements arriving during the battle Napoleon disposed of 190,000 men against a combined 335,000 allied troops

2 On 16 October Napoleon rebuffed the Army of Bohemia approaching from the south, but was unable to follow this up when the Army of Silesia attacked his positions from the northwest while Bennigsen's Russians theatened his left flank

3 On 17 October both sides regrouped. The Army of the North came into line between Blücher and Schwarzenberg, deploying in a huge semicircle east of the Elster

4 During 18 October the Allies launched six attacks against Napoleon who had pulled closer to the town, with Bertrand's corps cutting through to the west to secure a line of retreat. While putting up a stout defence, the Allies made progress in the north and northeast, the Saxons defected, losses were heavy and ammunition running low. The French position became untenabl

5 At 2 a.m. on 19 October Napoleon ordered a phased retreat. While a rearguard contested the Allied advances into the city, the bulk of his army managed to cross the one bridge over the Elster. But the bridge was blown too soon, compelling most of the rearguard to surrender. Although Allied losses of 54,000 were heavy, the victory enabled the Allied armies to advance to the Rhine

phased retreat to the west. At about noon his Saxon and Baden troops went over to the enemy, while the only bridge leading west out of the town was blown up prematurely, leaving some 50,000 troops trapped in the city.

Napoleon was forced to evacuate Germany. Bavarians and Austrians under General Wrede tried to intercept him east of Frankfurt at Hanau on 29–30 October, but were pushed aside. Only 70,000 men crossed the Rhine in formed units, 40,000 straggled in at various points and some 90,000 still held fortresses east of the Rhine. Another 100,000 were fighting Wellington in southern France. Exhaustion and sickness ravaged armies on both sides. The Allies halted their pursuit on the Rhine, undecided whether to invade France. Austria and Sweden were willing to settle more or less for the 'natural frontiers' of France, the Russians and the Prussians wanted to remove the 'Corsican Ogre' and England backed war to the end. Early in November Metternich offered Napoleon's representative a generous settlement, though it is not certain whether this offer had the consent of the other allies, especially England. But Napoleon delayed acceptance. When he was ready to do so, he found the offer withdrawn. Instead, on 22 December 1813, the allied armies began their invasion of France.

THE DEFENCE OF FRANCE: 1814

During the winter of 1813–14 Napoleon mustered yet another army, calling up 963,000 conscripts, pensioners, aged reservists, foresters, gendarmes, customs officers and the National Guard. He hoped that this great array, reminiscent of the levies of 1793–4, might give his opponents second thoughts about invading France. His expectations did not materialize. France was tired and only one in seven called up appeared. Yet he did gather 110,000 men, including 16-year-olds – *les Marie-Louises*. Defections continued. His German allies were gone, Westphalia had collapsed, the Dutch were in revolt. Early in January, Murat, allied with Austria and Denmark, deserted. Only Eugène remained loyal and managed to hold the Mincio line against Austrian and Neapolitan forces until Napoleon's abdication.

The 1814 campaign in France was as brilliant as any Napoleon had ever fought, while differences among the Allies continued to affect the campaign. Even so, while his strategy and tactics were brilliant and he managed to hold the adoration of his men, the campaign from the outset was hopeless. Napoleon deployed some 70,000 men in cordon to protect Paris, keeping a small army, only 30,000 to 40,000 men, to defeat the enemy armies individually. He remained, however, oblivious to the fact that France was tired and could not keep on fighting. Schwarzenberg planned to advance the Bohemian Army through Switzerland to the plateau of Langres, from where it could threaten Napoleon's communications, while the Army of Silesia would move through the Palatinate to Metz. Bernadotte's Army of the North was entering Belgium. All three armies incorporated Russian contingents. The Austrians and Prussians were to combine on the Marne to march on Paris. In essence, this was classic manoeuvre strategy, designed to avoid bloody action while exerting pressure on the enemy. Metternich still looked towards negotiations.

Schwarzenberg reached the Langres Plateau in late January 1814, only 50 kilometres separating him from Blücher. Here, however, Metternich instructed him to halt in order to permit a new diplomatic initiative. Napoleon seized the opportunity to fall on Blücher's 53,000-strong army near Brienne, and on 29 January pushed it back to La Rothière where, reinforced to 100,000 men by Schwarzenberg, Blücher repelled the French in two days. Overconfident, the united armies separated. Blücher's Prussian and Russian corps marched down the Marne on Paris, while Schwarzenberg delayed committing his army. Napoleon seized the opportunity. At Champaubert on 10 February, Montmirail on the 11th and Vauchamps on the 14th – three battles in five days –his corps mauled individual corps of Blücher's army, but did not destroy it. Even so, Napoleon had again demonstrated his superb

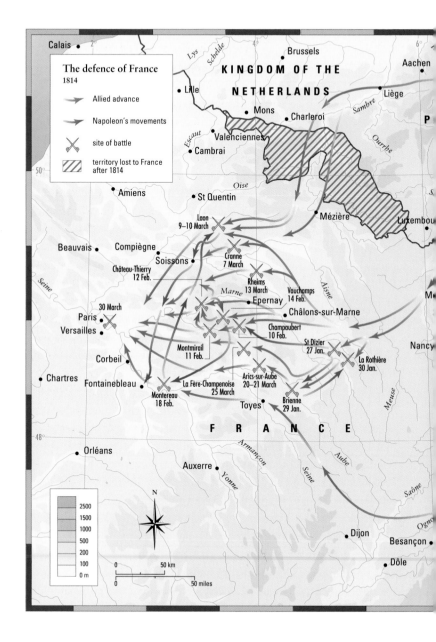

The defence of France
1814

→ Allied advance

→ Napoleon's movements

✕ site of battle

▨ territory lost to France after 1814

Calais
Lys
Schelde
Brussels
Aachen
KINGDOM OF THE
Lille
NETHERLANDS
Liège
Mons
Charleroi
Sambre
Valenciennes
Escaut
Cambrai
Ourthe
Mézière
Luxembou
Amiens
St Quentin
Oise
Beauvais
Compiègne
Laon
9–10 March
Soissons
Craonne
7 March
Château-Thierry
12 Feb.
Rheims
13 March
Vauchamps
14 Feb.
Marne
Epernay
Châlons-sur-Marne
Seine
30 March
Paris
Champaubert
10 Feb.
Versailles
St Dizier
27 Jan.
Corbeil
Montmirail
11 Feb.
Nancy
La Rothière
30 Jan.
Chartres
Fontainebleau
Arcis-sur-Aube
20–21 March
La Fère-Champenoise
25 March
Montereau
18 Feb.
Brienne
29 Jan.
Toyes
Meuse
F R A N C E
Orléans
Armançon
Seine
Aube
Auxerre
Yonne
Saône
2500
1500
1000
500
200
100
0 m
N
Dijon
Ogno
Besançon
0   50 km
0   50 miles
Dôle

skills, the morale of his tiny army soared and for the first time villagers turned out to cheer his passing troops.

He had hoped to continue after Blücher, but Schwarzenberg resumed his advance on Paris. Napoleon hurried south to the Seine and on 17–18 February at Monterau inflicted a serious setback on the Austrians, who, under orders to avoid risk, fell back on Troyes and beyond. At this point the Allies made another peace proposal, offering the boundaries of 1792. Napoleon refused. He exulted in his successes, distrusted the allied offer, believed in ultimate triumph and ignored the fact that his forces were dwindling, and that none of his victories had been decisive. Aware that Napoleon counted on allied dissension, on 1 March the powers signed the Treaty of Chaumont, pledging to fight until he was overthrown. The irrepressible Blücher resumed the offensive, pulling Napoleon north, but fell back when the emperor approached.

DEFENCE OF FRANCE, 1814

Hopeless from the outset, this campaign is considered among Napoleon's most skilful. As in his 1796 campaign, Napoleon used his interior position to attack the various converging allied armies individually, achieving some victories. Ultimately, of course, he could not prevent their superior numbers from threatening Paris, nor could he keep his marshals loyal.

In February 1814 the emperor and his staff, including Marshals Berthier and Ney, are riding towards another battle. Although Napoleon had recovered much of his old skills and his army, veterans and green recruits, fought gallantly, the odds against success were overwhelming and this campaign could not be won.

While Marmont was being defeated at the Heights of Montmartre, during the afternoon of 30 March 1814 General Moncey and National Guard troops made a brave if futile stand at the Porte de Clichy in Paris.

After a sharp engagement at Craonne, Blücher combined with his two reinforced corps at Laon, 140 kilometres north-east of Paris. Napoleon followed. On 9 March, before the French were ready, Blücher struck and with overwhelming numbers, 85,000 against 37,000, gained a pivotal victory. But Marmont, whose VI Corps was to be Napoleon's enveloping wing, had left the field to spend the night in comfort, so was absent when the Prussians attacked and smashed his corps. Napoleon had to retreat and never forgave Marmont for behaving like a 'second lieutenant'.

Napoleon retired to Soissons, assigning Marmont and Mortier to cover Paris, while, after smashing an isolated Prusso-Russian force at Rheims on 13 March, he turned against Schwarzenberg, then advancing towards Paris. On 20 March, with 30,000 men, he attacked 100,000 allies at Arcis-sur-Aube. Defeated, he staked everything on a last gamble. Leaving Marmont and Mortier to cover Paris, and instructing his brother Joseph to put the capital in a state of defence, he marched east to threaten allied communications with Germany, compelling them to withdraw their forces. Ignoring Napoleon's presence in their rear, the Allies saw their opportunity and directed the bulk of their combined armies, over 200,000 men, on Paris. Marmont and Mortier fought a bitter rearguard action at Fère-Champenoise on 25 March, retreated and, on the 30th, fought their last action on the Heights of Montmartre. During the night Marmont negotiated a local truce that enabled the Allies to occupy Paris, and five days later took his entire corps, some 11,000 men, into the allied camp. Napoleon's Foreign Minister Talleyrand had for some time been in touch with the Allies and welcomed a return of the Bourbons; Joseph, who had done nothing to defend the city, fled.

Napoleon, who had finally realized that his bluff was not working, headed for Paris on 27 March. He reached Fontainebleau on the 31st, just hours after Marmont's betrayal. Napoleon had one card left: the loyalty of the army. He still had about 36,000 men and could count on 60,000 within two days. Hoping to rally the country, he proposed to march on Paris. The soldiers and the regimental officers were willing to fight on, but the marshals and senior generals, eager to salvage their positions and wealth, and perhaps realistic, mutinied. On 3 April Talleyrand formed a provisional government in the capital, and the next day, the 4th, Napoleon was confronted by a group of marshals. With Ney taking the lead, Macdonald, Oudinot, Lefebvre and several other senior officers told the emperor that they refused to march. And when Napoleon asserted that the army would follow him, Ney replied, 'The army will only obey its generals.' Nothing more was left to be said. Napoleon abdicated on 6 April 1814 and was exiled to Elba.

CHAPTER SEVEN

The Waterloo Campaign 1815

At both Quatre Bras and Waterloo British
squares stood off French cavalry. Recounting
the battle of Waterloo to General Lord
Beresford, the Duke of Wellington wrote:
'I had the infantry for some time in squares
and we had French cavalry walking about us
as if they had been our own. I never saw the
British infantry behave so well!'

The Waterloo Campaign

T HE FOUR DAYS IN June constituting the Waterloo campaign may well be the most described military operation in history. It marked Napoleon's grand exit from the world stage and made Wellington a British legend. Given Napoleon's limited resources, including the decline of his own abilities and an unstable domestic base, he needed a rapid and conclusive victory to have any chance of staying in power. However, even if he had defeated Blücher and Wellington, in all probability this would not have caused the collapse of the coalition against him – it would only have prolonged his Hundred Days. In 1815 Napoleon's chances for ultimate success were even slimmer than in 1814.

NAPOLEON'S RETURN

On his abdication the Allies permitted Napoleon to retain his title, made him sovereign of the island of Elba, promised that the restored Bourbon monarchy would pay him an annual pension of 2 million francs and allowed 700 Old Guard volunteers to accompany him into exile. Napoleon arrived on Elba in early May 1814 and returned to France on 1 March 1815. In all, he spent not quite ten months on the island, keeping in close touch with the affairs of France and, after November, with the proceedings of the Congress of Vienna where Austria, Britain, Prussia and Russia struggled to redraw the map of Europe. He was well informed about French dissatisfaction with the Bourbon regime, the apprehensions of the peasantry, the discontent of the officers on half-pay and of the discharged veterans who could not find a place in society. Early in 1815 he received intelligence that the powers in Vienna had split into two hostile camps: Prussia and Russia against Austria and Britain. Finally, the Bourbons had refused to pay his pension and there were rumours that his removal to a more remote location was being contemplated.

Napoleon sailed for France on 26 February 1815, with 1,100 soldiers and four guns. Evading British naval patrols, the small force landed near Cannes and rapidly marched on Paris. Everywhere, troops sent to halt his advance came over to him. Louis XVIII fled into exile and on 20 March, without a shot fired, Napoleon entered Paris to the cheers of the populace. He announced that he desired only peace, but in Vienna news of his return quickly resolved inter-allied divisions. On 13 March the Allies had declared him an international outlaw and on 25 March formed a Seventh Coalition to which each of the four main powers promised to contribute 150,000 men. The minor states collectively pledged another 100,000. War had become Napoleon's only option to stay in power, and any remaining hope for a negotiated solution disappeared when, on 19 March, Murat, still king of Naples, attacked the Austrians in northern Italy, confirming the Allies' worst fears. In the event, Murat was badly defeated at Tolentino on 3 May, escaping to France where the emperor ignored his offer to serve.

THE ARMÉE DU NORD

Napoleon tried to reassure the Allies and the French people that his return meant peace and stability. To conciliate liberal opinion he continued the appointed Senate and the elected Chamber of Deputies, introduced by Louis XVIII, but he was under no illusion that his enemies would allow him to retain his throne. He expected that during the summer massive armies, perhaps of 650,000 or more, would attack France along its entire eastern frontier. To defend against these threats there was the standing army of 224,000 men, but with only 50,000 of them ready for field service. He raised additional manpower by recalling soldiers on half-pay and by a sizeable contingent of volunteers, repatriated prisoners of war and discharged veterans. Augmenting the volunteers were sailors from the fleet.

But this hardly was sufficient to produce an army large enough to withstand the expected allied invasion, and Napoleon tried to recall the 120,000 recruits of the class of 1815, most of whom had received some training in late 1813 or early 1814. But conscription had been abolished, and the Legislative Chamber, with the power to do so,

Europe after the Treaty of Vienna

German confederation

Iceland
to Denmark

0   200 km
0   200 miles

Norwegian Sea

Faeroe Islands to Denmark

Arctic Circle

N O R W A Y

S W E D E N

Finland

North Sea

Baltic Sea

RUSSIAN EMPIRE

Scotland
• Edinburgh

Copenhagen •
DENMARK

Hamburg

P R U S S I A

• Berlin

• Warsaw

REPUBLIC OF CRACOW

Ireland
Dublin •

GREAT BRITAIN

Amsterdam •
NETHERLANDS
Brussels •

HANOVER

PRUSSIA

Rhine

• Cracow

Wales

England
London •

SAXONY

• Prague

• Paris

BADEN
Stuttgart •
WÜRTTEMBERG

BAVARIA

Vienna

Hungary

Buda • Pest
•

ATLANTIC OCEAN

F R A N C E

Loire

NEUCHÂTEL
SWITZERLAND

A U S T R I A N   E M P I R E

Transylvania

Danube

MILITARY FRONTIERS

Moldavia

Wallachia

Bucharest •

SARDINIA

LOMBARDY
VENETIA

PARMA

• Genoa

MODENA

Zara •

OTTOMAN EMPIRE

Oporto •

ANDORRA

MASSA AND CARRARA

LUCCA

Florence •
TUSCANY

PAPAL STATES

Adriatic Sea

Montenegro

• Madrid

Corsica

Rome •

Aegean Sea

• Lisbon

PORT.

S P A I N

Balearic Is.

SARDINIA

Naples •

KINGDOM OF THE TWO SICILIES

Ionian Islands
to Great Britain

Athens •

• Gibraltar
to Great Britain

• Algiers

M e d i t e r

r a

n e a

Sicily

n   S e a

Crete

MOROCCO

ALGERIA

Tunis •

TUNIS

refused to recall the class of 1815. Napoleon circumvented the legislative by designating the class of 1815 as discharged soldiers who were obliged to serve, and by June some 46,000 of their number were on their way to the depots, though the war was over before any of them reached the field. In June 1815 Napoleon's army consisted almost entirely of old veterans and young volunteers, mostly fanatically loyal, but also brittle, suspicious of their leaders and prone to panic under pressure. To supplement these forces Napoleon called up National Guards for garrison and internal security duties.

The odds facing the emperor were formidable. Two allied armies – an Anglo-Dutch-German army under Wellington and a Prussian army under Blücher – were deployed in Belgium. Further to the south, along the Rhine, Prince Schwarzenberg was assembling a strong Austrian army, and 200,000 Russians were marching west from Poland. Napoleon resolved that he could not stand on the defensive and that his best, perhaps his only, chance, was to destroy the British and Prussian armies in Belgium, which might frighten the powers into a compromise peace. 'The Armée du Nord,' he told Davout who had been appointed minister of war, 'shall be the principal army,' and he decided to take personal command.

Finding sound senior subordinates proved difficult. Only six marshals were available for duty – Brune, Davout, Mortier, Ney, Soult and Suchet – the number rising to seven with the promotion of General Emmanuel

EUROPE AFTER THE TREATY OF VIENNA

Despite a number of serious disputes among the Allies, the Congress of Vienna completed re-mapping Europe and issued its final declaration on 8 June 1815. A Polish kingdom was created with the Tsar as king and some territories ceded to Austria and Prussia. Austria was restored to her former frontiers while Habsburg princes ruled Modena, Tuscany, and Parma. Prussia was enlarged, receiving Swedish Pomerania, half of Saxony, and substantial areas of the Rhineland. The German states, reduced in number to thirty-nine, were loosely united in a confederation. Belgium and the former Dutch Republic were united to form the Kingdom of the Netherlands. In Spain and Naples, the Bourbon rulers were reinstated.

Grouchy, a competent cavalry commander. Above all, the emperor missed Berthier. He had asked him to resume his old post, but Berthier had gone into exile where he died on 1 June, reportedly jumping to his death from a window in Bamberg. In his absence Napoleon appointed Soult, who lacked the qualifications required, as his chief of staff.

Remembering the bitter experience of the 1813 campaign when hard-won victories had been offset by defeats suffered by his independent subordinates, Napoleon was careful in his choice of commanders of the roughly 100,000-strong covering forces along the frontiers. The Army of the Rhine went to General Jean Rapp, Marshal Suchet received the Army of the Alps, Marshal Brune the Army of the Var and General Clausel was entrusted with the forces on the Spanish frontier. Davout's appointment remains questionable. The most able among the marshals, the only one with proven capability for independent command, Davout became Minister of War and Governor of Paris. He did a superb job preparing the Armée du Nord, but once the campaign opened his presence in the field might have changed the outcome, while his presence in Paris was of little consequence if the emperor was victorious, and could change nothing if he was beaten.

After deducting covering forces Napoleon's main army numbered some 123,000 combatants, the Imperial Guard, five army corps and the cavalry reserve, supported by 358 pieces of ordnance. The Armée du Nord was organized into two wings and a reserve. The reserve – basically the 20,000-strong Guard, initially commanded by Mortier, but after he fell ill by General Drouot – was intended to reinforce either wing as necessary. Given Napoleon's strategic intent, the wing commands were crucial assignments, but he decided on their commanders only after the army had already invaded Belgium.

NAPOLEON'S WAR PLAN

As far back as March Napoleon had decided that he could not wait for the Allies to attack, but, estimating that they would be ready after 1 July, he determined to pre-empt them by falling on the Anglo-Dutch and

Prussian armies in Belgium. In June these two armies were dispersed in an area 145 kilometres long and about 45 kilometres deep. Wellington, with 107,000 Anglo-Dutch-Germans, held the western half of Belgium from the Brussels–Charleroi road to the Scheldt river; to the east, Blücher, with 149,000 Prussians, occupied the country to the Meuse river. Their lines of communications diverged. Wellington's ran north and west towards Ostend, Blücher's through Namur east into Germany. Aware that the allied armies had a two-to-one numerical superiority, Napoleon planned to concentrate his army secretly one day's march from Charleroi just south of the hinge of the two allied armies. Then, striking swiftly before the enemy could concentrate his dispersed forces, he intended to drive a wedge between the two armies, hoping that each would fall back to protect its communications; then he could defeat each in turn.

On 3 June Napoleon issued orders for the concentration of the Armée du Nord. By the night of 14 June he had massed his whole force on a 24-kilometre front within striking distance of Charleroi, without the Allies becoming aware of the extent of the threat. The concentration had been well executed, though as late as 12 June Grouchy's four-division cavalry corps had not received its marching orders. The cavalry caught up and concentration was not delayed, but Napoleon should have been alerted to Soult's sloppy staff work. None the less, he had achieved strategic and operational surprise and was within a day's march of the juncture between the British and Prussian forces – the intersection at Quatre Bras on the Brussels–Charleroi road. The next day, 15 June, its frontage reduced to only 10 kilometres, the army crossed into Belgium.

That afternoon Napoleon finally appointed wing commanders. He gave Ney command of the left wing: I and II Corps. Napoleon must have realized that Ney was incapable of independent command, but also knew that the rank and file adored him. He may have hoped that the marshal would comply with written instructions; as it turned out, Ney ignored their intent. The right wing – III and IV Corps – went to Grouchy, a talented cavalry commander, but without combined arms experience and lacking seniority. Davout would have been a better choice than Ney, and Suchet, whose forces actually threw back an Austrian offensive on the Rhine, would have been better than Grouchy. Ney was ordered towards Quatre Bras, though his orders did not specify the need to seize the intersection, while Grouchy was directed towards Sombreffe. Napoleon retained the Guard, the cavalry reserve and VI Corp under his direct control.

THE ALLIED ARMIES AND THEIR PLANS

The two allied armies in Belgium had been hastily built up from the original occupation forces. Both lacked their best formations and contained elements whose reliability was in doubt. The British had shipped many of their regulars to fight in North America, and when Wellington returned to Brussels in April he was disturbed both by the quality and numbers of his composite forces assembling there – 'a most infamous army'. By June his strength had risen to about 93,000 men, with 79,000 in his field force, of which, however, only one-third was British. A majority of the senior officers and about half of the men in the British and King's German Legion units had served with him in the Peninsula. The newly founded Kingdom of the Netherlands, combining Belgium and Holland, provided about 16,000 men, many of whom had served Napoleon. In addition there were some 15,000 Hanoverian *Landwehr* and contingents from Nassau and Brunswick. Altogether the force had 197 guns.

Wellington's army was organized into two infantry, one cavalry and a reserve corps: the young Prince of Orange commanded I Corps – two Dutch-Belgian and two British divisions; II Corps – three divisions – was under Lieutenant General Lord Hill; the cavalry was commanded by General Paget, Earl of Uxbridge. Wellington retained control of the 25,000-strong reserve – two British divisions and the Brunswick and Nassau contingents.

The Prussian Army of the Lower Rhine had been reinforced to 117,000 men and 296 guns, including 9,000 Saxons who had mutinied in May, as well as Rhinelanders who were not fond of their new masters. The army was organized into four combined arms corps, with Ziethen's I Corps deployed as an advance guard in the Fleurus–Charleroi area. While Wellington rarely held a high opinion of his allies, he liked and trusted Blücher. The two commanders met on 3 June and agreed that if the French attacked, Wellington would concentrate his army towards the Prussians, a contingency plan he initially failed to implement, almost wrecking the allied campaign.

In the absence of declared war, the Allies had not conducted mounted reconnaissance across the frontier, but Blücher received sighting reports on the 14th, and a defecting French divisional commander, General Bourmont, confirmed that Napoleon would attack at Charleroi. On 15 June the Prussian staff began to move its remaining three corps forward to concentrate at Ligny and Sombreffe, placing them directly in the path of Napoleon's right wing. But Wellington did not act until the afternoon of 15 June. Convinced that Napoleon planned to cut him off from the Channel ports, he ordered his entire army to shift west towards Mons, uncovering the vital Quatre Bras area and placing Blücher's deployment in peril. Only at 1 a.m. on the 16th did he realize that the enemy was coming from Charleroi – in his words he had been 'humbugged' by Napoleon – and he began to hurry troops down to Quatre Bras. It is hard to find a convincing explanation for Wellington's initial reaction. Napoleon wanted to separate the Allies, who outnumbered him two to one, and would not have attacked the British right flank because this would have pushed them in on the Prussians. Wellington and Blücher were saved because a brilliant Napoleonic plan foundered on irresolute commanders, and poor staff work and inadequate communications.

LIGNY AND QUATRE BRAS: 16 JUNE
The Waterloo campaign included three major battles fought within a period of three days. Two of these took place on 16 June, the second

Ligny and Quatre Bras
About 14.00 hrs, 16 June 1815

→ French advance

→ Allied advance

⬭ French concentration

Ligny and Quatre bras

Napoleon had managed to gain strategic surprise; by early afternoon on 16 June his army, in two wings, had almost placed itself between Wellington's and Blücher's armies. While Napoleon pressed against the Prussians at Ligny, Ney was to seize Quatre Bras and envelop Blücher.

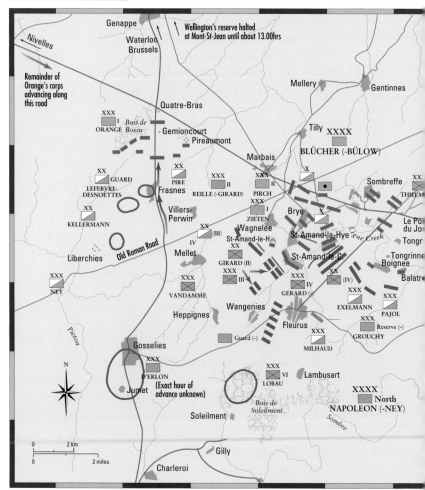

day of the invasion. Joining Grouchy, Napoleon fought Blücher at Ligny, while Ney tried to capture the crossroads at Quatre Bras.

Quatre Bras, Ligny and Charleroi form an inverted triangle, its corners connected by main roads. Although delayed for several hours by an administrative mistake, the French swept through Charleroi, but

then slowed down. By afternoon Grouchy had pushed Ziethen to just outside Fleurus, but halted there. Ney had done no better. By late afternoon he had advanced only 7 kilometres beyond Charleroi. He could have captured Quatre Bras the first evening, but, cautious for the first time in his career and with only II Corps in action, he hesitated. As it was, during the afternoon General de Rebeque, the Prince of Orange's chief of staff, in an intelligent disobedience of orders to shift his divisions west, had authorized his 2nd Division to send a brigade into Quatre Bras, and during the night reinforced it with a second brigade. The next morning Ney still outnumbered the defenders six to one, but failed to act.

Even so, early on 16 June the situation favoured Napoleon who decided to envelop and destroy Blücher. He did not know the numbers of troops Wellington was pushing to Quatre Bras, but saw that Blücher's position at Ligny was dangerously exposed to envelopment by Ney. Late in the morning he issued new orders to Ney. After seizing Quatre Bras, the marshal was to swing the bulk of his corps down the road to Ligny against Blücher's flank and rear, while the emperor and Grouchy attacked frontally. Rapid responses to changing situations were fundamental to Napoleonic battle tactics, but Soult was slow to formulate and transmit clear orders. Having wasted the morning, Ney received

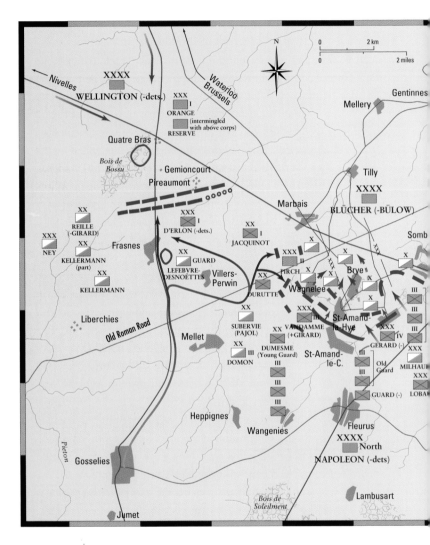

During the night Wellington had rushed reinforcements to Quatre Bras, but Ney failed to react energetically. By noon, realizing that Ney would not arrive in time, Napoleon had mounted a frontal attack against the Prussians that, after the Guard was committed, drove them back by nightfall. It was the emperor's last victory.

Ligny and Quatre Bras
21.00 hrs, 16 June 1815

→ French advance

→ Allied advance

⇢ Allied retreat

◯ French concentration

◯ Allied concentration

XXX
IV
BÜLOW

Corroy-le-
Château

XXX
III
ELMANN

Le Pont
du Jour

Tongrinne
X
Mazy

XXX
PAJOL Balatre
(BER VIE)

XXX
LMANN

XXX
IV
ROUCHY

L'Omeau

Sombre

instructions to take Quatre Bras and then wheel against Blücher only in mid afternoon.

Soon after noon Wellington had arrived on the scene and conferred with Blücher, promising to send him at least one corps. Then he returned to Quatre Bras where, with more reinforcements arriving, he achieved parity, later superiority, against Ney. Ney, reacting to his new instructions, decided to take his objective with his second major formation, d'Erlon's I Corps, then moving up from Charleroi. But by a staff slip-up he had not been notified that Napoleon had ordered this corps to be diverted to attack Blücher's right at Ligny. Enraged, Ney recalled the corps with the result that its 20,000 men spent the afternoon marching and countermarching, without coming into action, a mix-up which may have cost Napoleon the battle. Meanwhile, Ney himself led repeated charges against the British, now numbering 31,000 men; when darkness ended the fighting Wellington firmly held the crossroads.

The battle of Ligny was a larger affair. By noon, along a 10-kilometre front either side of Ligny, Blücher had deployed three corps, a rather larger number than Napoleon, who had left VI Corps behind at Charleroi, had expected. Napoleon wanted to pin the Prussians by a frontal assault, while Ney struck their exposed right and rear. Aware that Ney had not taken Quatre Bras, at about 3.15 p.m. he decided to employ d'Erlon's corps to attack the Prussian flank, but neglected to inform the marshal of his decision. Moreover, when some of d'Erlon's troops approached from an unexpected direction Grouchy's left flank division panicked, requiring Napoleon's personal intervention to restore stability. With the flank attack a fiasco, the emperor unleashed his Guard and by 8 p.m. the Prussian line was broken. A mounted counter-attack, which Blücher led in person, failed. Unhorsed, the field marshal was out of touch with his headquarters for several hours, but his chief of staff, von Gneisenau, took over. Shielded by darkness and heavy rain, having lost 16,000 men and 21 guns, the Prussians withdrew in fair order.

Ligny was Napoleon's last victory, but the failure of the *manoeuvre sur les derrières* allowed the Prussians to escape. Physically and mentally exhausted, and still in the dark about the situation at Quatre Bras, he failed to order an immediate pursuit. At 8 a.m. the next morning he again instructed Ney to take Quatre Bras, but then delayed another three hours before ordering him to make an all-out effort. Napoleon's dilatory actions on the morning of 17 June lost his last chance to attack Wellington while he was isolated. If Ney had pinned Wellington at Quatre Bras the exposed British left flank would have been vulnerable to a thrust down the road from Ligny, but the emperor did not exploit the opportunity. That morning Wellington received Blücher's promise that he would support him with two corps, and only began to disengage his infantry at 10 a.m. Under cover of a heavy thunderstorm and protected by a mounted rearguard, the British fell back to the ridge of Mont St Jean, 20 kilometres to the north.

During the night Blücher had rejoined his staff and decided to retreat north to Wavre rather than east to Namur. This meant that he could maintain his link with Wellington and deliver the promised support. To prevent this, late in the morning, Napoleon had detached Grouchy with 33,000 men to shadow Blücher and prevent his junction with Wellington, while sending the Guard to Quatre Bras. When Napoleon joined Ney at about 2 p.m. he berated him for his inaction, but Wellington was gone. Pursuit finally got under way in the afternoon. However, slowed by heavy rain and muddy ground, the French failed to catch up with the British.

Waterloo: the final defeat

On the morning of 18 June Napoleon with 74,000 men faced Wellington with 67,000. Wellington's main position ran along a low, 7-kilometre-wide ridge, allowing a heavy defensive concentration that made enemy breakthroughs extremely difficult. He positioned the bulk of his infantry – units of I and II Corps deliberately interspersed – just behind the crest of the ridge. Only one Netherlands' brigade near the centre was mistakenly posted on the forward slope. There were two major fortified outposts: on the right was the Château du Hougoumont, to the centre-left the walled farm of La Haye-Sainte. These strongpoints could be taken only at heavy cost, and if bypassed would unbalance the assault. Artillery was dispersed to provide direct fire support, while the cavalry stood massed behind the centre. The only flaw in Wellington's disposition was that, fixated on a line of retreat to the coast, he had posted 17,000 troops at Hale, 13 kilometres to his right; though desperately needed during the battle, they did not see action.

Napoleon never seriously considered outflanking the position. He had driven the Prussians away and, at least momentarily, split the Allies. Now he needed a quick victory which required a frontal attack breaking through the enemy centre. His army was drawn up in three lines. Reille's II Corps on the left and d'Erlon's I Corps on the right formed the first line, massed cavalry behind their flanks with Lobau's VI Corps in the centre provided the second line, while the Guard and more cavalry constituted the third line. Napoleon planned for Reille to launch a diversion and take Hougoumont with parts of his corps, while, following bombardment by an 80-gun grand battery, d'Erlon's four divisions were to penetrate the British centre. Then the cavalry and the second and third lines were to be unleashed to exploit the rupture and complete the destruction of the enemy.

Inexplicably, considering the incompetence demonstrated in 1813 and even more so during the previous two days, the emperor, who was far from well, gave Ney tactical charge of the battle. Normally Napoleon opened his battles at dawn, but, being confident that Grouchy would keep Blücher away, he delayed his attack until the muddy ground had dried enough to get his 12-pounders into position. Fighting began at about 11.30 a.m. with the attack against Hougoumont. The assault failed to draw reserves away from Wellington's centre, escalating into a

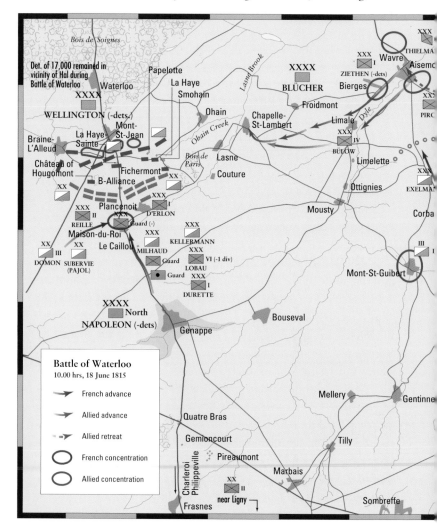

major engagement which absorbed several divisions. Napoleon's main effort opened an hour later when the grand battery blasted Wellington's position to little effect. Then, at about 2 p.m., d'Erlon's corps lurched forwards in four heavy columns towards La Haye-Sainte and the British centre. Bypassing La Haye-Sainte, the columns were stopped by British volleys and then flung back by a cavalry charge. D'Erlon's corps was badly mauled, but the British cavalry failed to rally in time and, taken in the flank by French lancers, suffered heavy casualties.

At about 1 p.m., even before d'Erlon's attack, the French had sighted troops approaching from the north-east, soon confirmed as Prussians. Earlier that day

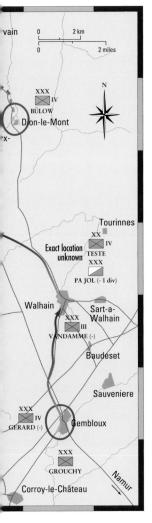

BATTLE OF WATERLOO

The British had fallen back to their new position on the reverse slope of the ridge of Saint Jean straddling the highway to Brussels. They deployed in linear order, but several lines deep, with fortified outposts at the Chateau of Hougomont and on the farm of La Haye-Sainte. It had rained heavily on the 17th, both sides were exhausted and soaked and the ground was muddy, delaying the deployment of Napoleon's grand battery until about 10 a.m. Ill that day, Napoleon gave Ney command of the battle and intervened only sporadically. At about 10 30 a.m. fighting began with an attack against Wellington's right, but the main attack was directed against the British centre and left by d'Erlon's corps. By 2 p.m. both attacks had stalled. Soon after scouts reported Prussian troops from the east. Grouchy, dispatched the day before to follow Blücher, had been halted at Wavre, while the Prussian, as promised, marched west to support Wellington. By 4 p.m. Prussian advance forces came in on Napoleon's left flank.

Grouchy had informed Napoleon that he was pursuing the Prussians towards Wavre, and in return had received instructions to block Blücher and join the French right flank. The orders seemed contradictory and Grouchy, displaying little imagination or common sense, took the

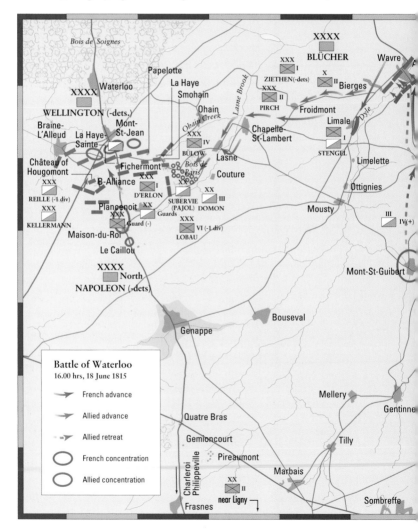

admittedly confusing orders literally and continued to press against the Prussian rearguard at Wavre even though he could hear the cannon at Waterloo. Meanwhile, delayed by poor roads and muddy terrain, Blücher continued his march to fall on Napoleon's right flank.

Under other circumstances Napoleon might have called off the battle as the odds increasingly turned against him, but he knew that without the advantage of initial surprise he could never again hope to split the allied armies. Realizing that Grouchy would not arrive, and with time running out, at 3 p.m. he ordered an all-out assault to take La Haye-Sainte. During the preliminary bombardment Wellington made a minor adjustment in position, mistaken by Ney for a major withdrawal, who threw forward two cavalry divisions forcing Wellington's infantry to form squares. Unsupported by infantry or artillery, an allied counatercharge drove the French back. Ney now committed his last mounted units, including the Guard cavalry, but again the charge was decimated by artillery and repelled by the steady squares.

By this time Napoleon was preoccupied. On his right the Prussians had reached the village of Planchenoit, compelling VI Corps which had advanced to refuse its line. At about 6 p.m. Ney finally took La Haye-Sainte and brought up artillery to batter the British positions. But Napoleon was unable to give him troops to exploit the success. Except for fifteen battalions of the Old Guard and eight of the Young Guard, the

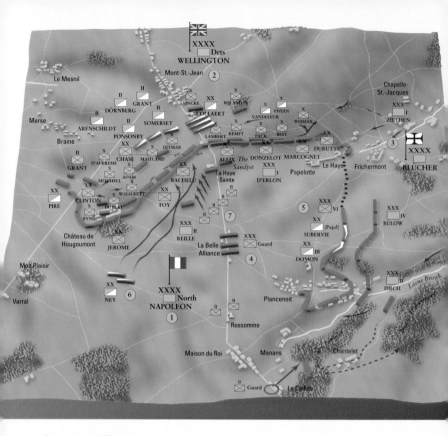

Battle of Waterloo

1 Napoleon displayed little energy during his last campaign. Detatching Marshal Grouchy with about one third of his army to contain the defeated Blücher, he slowly follows the British withdrawal north

2 Wellington decides to stand on a ridge near Mont St Jean, packing his 68,000 British, Dutch–Belgian and German troops in dense formation on a downhill slope

3 He is further encouraged by Blücher's promise to come to his aid with at least one corps by noon of 19 June. Grouchy is supposed to prevent this but sticks to the letter of his poorly worded instructions. Rain-soaked ground delays deployment of the heavy French artillery which comes at only about 1 pm. Meanwhile the French launch a diversionary attack against the Château de Hougoumont

4 Covered by heavy bombardment the French army deploys to attack, but the various attacks are poorly handled with little co-ordination between infantry, cavalry and artillery. Meanwhile, off to the north-east, the Prussian advance guard is sighted

5 Napoleon now has to detach one corps to face the Prussians, another corps already fighting around Hougoumont. Lacking infantry Ney, misreading an adjustment in the British line, orders unsupported cavalry charges at about 3 pm

6 When these fail Napoleon orders Ney to capture La Haye Sainte, the key to Wellington's centre. By 6 pm Ney succeeds but lacks infantry to exploit his success. Napoleon still has some twelve battalions of his Guard but hesitates to send them in

7 He releases them to Ney about 7 pm but they are beaten back. At this point, with several Prussian corps in action, the French army breaks and routs from the field

emperor had no more reserves. On his right more Prussians came into action to capture Planchenoit from Lobau. After the Young Guard retook the village, only to lose it again, Napoleon sent in two Old Guard battalions that captured and held the village, temporarily stabilizing the French right flank.

But with elements of three Prussian corps in action Napoleon threw in his last reserve, himself leading eleven Old Guard battalions to Ney, leaving behind one battalion as a personal escort and another at La Haye-Sainte to anchor a repulse. Shortly after 7 p.m. Ney once again displayed his personal bravery leading the final attack, with six battalions in the first and five in the second line, all formed in sixty-men-abreast battalion columns. Again, British and Dutch infantry rose to deliver their deadly short-range volleys. For the first time in its career the Old Guard wavered and then broke. Its repulse was the last straw for the French line troops who had fought well all day. Seeing the defeat of the supposedly invincible Guard, the other units were seized with near panic and, except for two battalions of Old Guard grenadiers, began to disintegrate. As the allied armies merged at about 9 p.m. Wellington ordered a general advance, Wellington meeting Blücher at the well-named coach inn 'La Belle Alliance', on the road to Charleroi.

On the right VI Corps held long enough to let the Armée du Nord escape on the road to Charleroi. But Napoleon had fought his last battle. He made it back to his escort Guard battalion, then to Charleroi and by coach to Paris. On the 19th he wrote to his brother Joseph that he could still collect 150,000 men to continue the war, but in Paris the legislature refused to support him and his ministers were preparing to disavow him. His brother, Lucien, and Davout urged him to dissolve the legislature and proclaim himself a dictator, but, as in 1814, he declined to call on the Parisian lower classes to rise in his defence. He also refused to join the army Davout was regrouping beyond the Loire. Both courses of action would have precipitated civil war, and a tired Napoleon no longer had the stomach for such a bloody affair. On 22 June he signed his second abdication. The Napoleonic Wars were over.

Epilogue: Napoleon's system of war – the pursuit of the decisive battle

THE ALMOST CONTINUOUS WARS between 1792 and 1815 transformed warfare. This transformation was not the result of major technological innovations. All armies employed pre-existing weapons and adopted improvements made by others. The great transformation in war came about because of the expanded scale of resources devoted to war. With the increase in Europe's military potential – more men, more food, more metals, improved roads and better maps – the congruence of the French Revolution and the early stages of the Industrial Revolution enabled governments to raise huge armies, armed and equipped by new industrial processes. At Valmy the forces of both sides together mustered fewer than 100,000; at Leipzig the opposing armies numbered well over a million.

This increase had operational and strategic consequences. Before 1792 commanders sought to avoid battle; the generals of the Revolution and Napoleon pursued it eagerly. Once expensive and hard to replace, soldiers had become cheap and replacements easy to procure. Mass placed a premium on the attack, making rapid decisions both essential and possible. Yet, the means of supplying armies had not changed. Even in the most fertile parts of Europe, living off the land, by no means a totally new practice, could only provide rations and forage for vast numbers of men and horses for a limited time. Unless there was a quick victory allowing them to move into unspoiled areas, armies had to disperse to live and concentrate to fight.

During the first phase of the Revolutionary–Napoleonic Wars, 1792–1807, the French armies and the Grande Armée enjoyed a distinctive advantage in force structure, strategy and tactics against more traditional opponents. Initially, this advantage increased when, after Napoleon's seizure of power, all policy-making – domestic, foreign and military – was concentrated in one hand. To Napoleon, for whom moderation had no meaning and who looked for hegemony in Europe and perhaps beyond, war was not the ultimate step to be taken when diplomacy failed, it was the central element of his foreign policy. To pursue his objective Napoleon favoured short offensive campaigns, designed to destroy the enemy's main army, and compel the defeated to accept his terms. His tactics tended to conform to his strategy, and the assault columns, massed mounted charges and grand batteries were not so much evidence of the declining quality of his army – though decline there was – but instruments to achieve the quick results required by a mass army.

He achieved many brilliant victories, but decisive, war-ending victories were few and their results not permanent. Only Austerlitz, Friedland and Wagram compelled his opponents to seek peace, though a few years later their military posture improved and, with promises of help from allies, they challenged the imposed peace treaties. Moreover, even decisive victories did not always produce the desired political result. The twin victories at Jena and Auerstädt did not extinguish Prussian resistance for another eight months. In fact, the 'glory years' during which Napoleon was unequalled as a strategist and field commander were quite short, the period 1805 to 1809.

From 1809 Napoleon's system no longer produced crushing victories, destroying opposing armies. There were a number of reasons for this. As his opponents realized his boundless ambitions, their political will stiffened and they made ever-greater efforts to defeat him. Although only Prussia introduced conscription, Austria, Russia,and Britain increased the size of their armies and eroded Napoleon's manpower advantage. Individually, their armies were still smaller than the French, but, when operated according to a common plan, they outnumbered them. Yet perhaps more important, all powers introduced corps as the main manoeuvre element, improved staff work and adopted tactics similar to the French. Even if imperfect in practice, their corps structure enhanced command and control and made Napoleon's opponents more resilient in defeat. His success had always depended on a strategy that forced the adversary to conform to his plan and to accept a decisive battle. But if the enemy could avoid this and was prepared to trade space for time, then Napoleon was in trouble. In 1809 he defeated the Austrians but did not destroy their army, though their political will failed, while, simultaneously, British forces and Spanish guerrillas began the long Peninsular war, ultimately tying down a third of his total available forces. Napoleon did not need Spain and he could have continued his accommodation with Russia, but he was never willing to make concessions and overreached himself.

His system became too centralized and at the same time extended too far. He insisted on sole control of planning and operations and did not allow his staff any independent role. His solution to the problem of how to combine central command and dispersal – the corps system –

Trying to stabilize his army and allow for an orderly retreat, Napoleon personally deployed the last remaining units of the Old Guard and remained with them until the most pressing crisis was over. Then he and his escort made for Gemappes, where he vainly hoped to reform his defeated army.

placed heavy demands on the administrative, tactical and even strategic competence of his senior subordinates. Napoleon made no systematic effort to instruct these men in higher military thought or to inform them of his plans. This worked as long as the emperor was close, but as his army was committed to fight from Spain to Russia, and grew from a few corps to army groups, his strategic control collapsed. Increasingly, his subordinates had to make their own decisions, and in 1809, 1812 and all subsequent campaigns some senior commanders failed to understand or carry out Napoleon's orders and intent.

At his best no general facing him was quite his equal – not Blücher, Archduke Charles, Kutuzov or Wellington – but from 1807 there were a series of setbacks which indicated that he could be defeated. Yet Napoleon should not be underrated. Few understood as well as he the possibilities and limitations of time and space, and few commanders had his ability to inspire devotion and courage amidst peril and confusion. To be sure, his physical and mental abilities seemed in decline after 1809, though there were occasional flashes of brilliance, but he remained formidable even in eclipse. Like most military institutions Napoleon's army was to a large degree the product of its historical experience, transformed and made more powerful by the charismatic genius of its leader. Wellington, for one, held that Napoleon's presence on the battlefield was worth 40,000 men, not only because of his tactical genius but because he inspired all ranks to do their utmost. As it was, his army served him well, sometimes better than he deserved, and even in adversity the hard core of the army remained loyal to him.

It has been argued that the wars of Napoleon represented the most intensive exploitation of the manpower, technology and logistic capabilities of his time, but that they signalled the end of an era of classical warfare and not the beginning of a new era of modern war. Perhaps, yet despite enormous changes in technology, many campaigns and battles since 1815 have been fought on the Napoleonic pattern, and Napoleon's campaigns continue to form part of the curriculum at advanced military schools throughout the world.

Biographical notes

Alexander I

ALEXANDER I, TSAR OF RUSSIA (1777–1825)
Participated in the Third Coalition but co-operated with Napoleon after 1807; in 1812, however, he refused to treat after the loss of Moscow and joined the Sixth Coalition 1813.

ALVINCZY, GENERAL JOSEPH, BARON (1735–1805)
Austrian commander defeated at Arcola and Rivoli.

AUGEREAU, MARSHAL PIERRE-FRANÇOIS-CHARLES (1757–1816)
As general of division he gained fame at Castiglione; he was created marshal 1804 and led corps at Jena and Eylau.

BACLER D'ALBE, BRIGADIER GENERAL LOUIS ALBERT (1761–1824)
Headed Napoleon's topographical office from 1804.

BAGRATION, GENERAL PETER (1765–1812)
He served under Suvorov 1799; commanded rearguard 1805; he fought at Austerlitz, Eylau and Friedland and was mortally wounded at Borodino.

BARCLAY DE TOLLY, FIELD MARSHAL MIKHAIL, PRINCE (1761–1818)
A good administrator, minister of war since 1810, he modernized the Russian Army; an indifferent field commander 1812, he was replaced by Kutuzov.

BEAUHARNAIS, VICEROY EUGÈNE DE (1781–1824)
Napoleon's stepson; an able soldier, viceroy of Italy 1805; distinguished at Wagram, Borodino and during retreat from Moscow; in 1815 effectively defended Italy.

BENNIGSEN, GENERAL LEVIN (1753–1826)
Russian commander at Eylau; he fought at Borodino and Leipzig.

BERESFORD, GENERAL WILLIAM CARR (1764–1854)
He retrained and commanded the Portuguese Army from 1809 to 1812.

BERNADOTTE, MARSHAL JEAN-BAPTISTE, KING OF SWEDEN (1763–1844)
Created marshal in 1804, he did well in 1805, but after questionable conduct at Jena and Wagram was dismissed from the army; Crown Prince of Sweden from 1810, he commanded the Army of the North against Napoleon in 1813.

BERTHIER, MARSHAL LOUIS-ALEXANDRE (1753–1815)
Napoleon's indispensable chief of staff 1798–1814; promoted marshal 1804; committed suicide 1815.

BESSIÈRES, MARSHAL JEAN-BAPTISTE (1768–1813)
A distinguished cavalry commander, marshal 1804, he fought at Austerlitz, Jena, Eylau, Friedland, Aspern–Essling and Wagram; killed in action Germany, May 1813.

BLÜCHER, FIELD MARSHAL GEBHARD LEBERECHT VON (1742–1819)
Brave, energetic, if intellectually limited; formed effective command team with Gneisenau 1813–14; commanded Prussian Army in Belgium 1815; defeated at Ligny, he provided critical support to Wellington at Waterloo.

BONAPARTE, JEROME, KING OF WESTPHALIA (1784–1860)
Napoleon's youngest brother; became king 1807; relieved of command in Russia, but supported his brother in 1815 and fought at Waterloo.

Jérôme Bonaparte

BONAPARTE, JOSEPH, KING OF NAPLES, THEN OF SPAIN (1768–1844)
Napoleon's elder brother became King of Naples 1806; abdicated in
favour of Murat to become King of Spain 1808.

BRUNSWICK, GENERAL CARL WILHELM FERDINAND, DUKE (1735–1806)
A veteran Prussian general repulsed at Valmy; he was killed
commanding the Prussian Army at Auerstädt.

BUXHÖWDEN, FIELD MARSHAL FRIEDRICH WILHELM (1750–1811)
He was lieutenant-general in command of the first three columns of
the Allied army in the failed Austro-Russian attack at Austerlitz.

CARNOT, GENERAL LAZARE (1753–1823)
Politician, the 'organizer of victory', member Committee of Public
Safety, he reorganized and directed the French
Republican armies.

**CHARLES, FIELD MARSHAL, ARCHDUKE OF
AUSTRIA** (1771–1847)
Ablest Habsburg general, he defeated the
French in Germany 1796 and repulsed
Napoleon at Aspern–Essling 1809; his
efforts to overhaul the Austrian Army had
only limited success; he was removed from
command after Wagram.

Field Marshal Charles

CLAUSEWITZ, GENERAL CARL VON
(1780–1831)
Prussian staff officer, commentator on Napoleonic Wars, celebrated
for his still influential work *On War*.

DAVOUT, MARSHAL LOUIS-NICOLAS (1770–1823)
Napoleon's ablest and most loyal marshal appointed 1804; he gained
fame at Auerstädt and commanded corps with distinction thereafter;
Minister of War 1815.

DESAIX, GENERAL LOUIS-CHARLES (1768–1800)
Was with Bonaparte in Egypt; he was killed
leading the decisive charge at Marengo.

DUMOURIEZ, GENERAL CHARLES-FRANÇOIS
(1739–1823)
He shared credit for Valmy; victor at
Jemappes, but defected to the Allies in
1793.

General Louis-Charles Desaix

**FERDINAND, PRINCE OF ASTURIAS,
KING OF SPAIN** (1784–1833)
Involved in constitutional crisis of 1808 leading to the French
occupation of Spain.

FRANCIS I, EMPEROR OF AUSTRIA (1768–1835)
A mediocre reactionary ruler, unwilling to support strongly his brother
Charles; his daughter Marie-Louise married Napoleon in 1808.

FREDERICK WILLIAM III, KING OF PRUSSIA (1770–1840)
Engaged Napoleon 1806; massively defeated, he
became a French client ruler; joined Sixth
Coalition 1813.

GNEISENAU, GENERAL AUGUSTUS WILHELM
(1760–1831)
Defended Kolberg 1806, then helped
Prussian army reforms; intellectual
partner of Blücher's command team
1813–15.

GRIBEAUVAL, JEAN-BAPTISTE, COUNT
(**1715–1789**)
After 1765 he restructured French artillery,
designing a range of mobile pieces.

*General Augustus
Wilhelm Gneisenau*

GROUCHY, MARSHAL EMMANUEL DE (1766–1847)
Capable cavalry leader, promoted beyond his ability to marshal
April 1815; he was assigned command of right wing of the
Armée du Nord.

GUIBERT, GENERAL JACQUES-ANTOINE DE (1743–90)
Military philosopher, his writings had considerable influence on
Enlightenment military thought.

HILL, GENERAL SIR ROWLAND (1772–1842)
In Peninsula led division at Talavera 1809;
commanded First Allied Corps at Waterloo.

HOCHE, GENERAL LAZARE (1768–97)
Rose to general of division 1793; commanded
Army of the Moselle; led abortive expedition
to Ireland 1796, and Army of Sambre and
Meuse 1797.

General Lazare Hoche

**HOHENLOHE, GENERAL FRIEDRICH LUDWIG,
PRINCE OF** (1746–1818)
Massively defeated at Jena 1806 and forced to surrender following
long retreat.

JOHN, ARCHDUKE OF AUSTRIA (1782–1859)
Defeated at Hohenlinden; he commanded in Italy and Hungary in
1809, but failed to join Charles at Wagram.

JOURDAN, MARSHAL JEAN-BAPTISTE (1762–1833)
General of division 1793; victor at Fleurus 1794; instrumental in passing
conscription law 1798; promoted marshal 1804; he served in Spain.

KLEBER, GENERAL JEAN-BAPTISTE (1753–1800)
Commanded in Egypt after Napoleon's departure; maintained
French position until assassinated.

KRAY, GENERAL PAUL (1735–1804)
Old Austrian veteran commander, he served in Italy and Germany 1800.

KUTUZOV, FIELD MARSHAL MIKHAIL (1745–1813)
Commanded Russian army in Germany 1805, was pressured to attack at Austerlitz; defeated at Borodino 1812 but kept army in existence.

LANNES, MARSHAL JEAN (1769–1809)
A great fighting soldier, appointed marshal 1804, distinguished himself at Aspern–Essling where he was mortally wounded.

LEFEBVRE, MARSHAL FRANÇOIS-JOSEPH (1755–1820)
A blunt soldier who rose from sergeant major to marshal by 1804; a poor strategist, he was a fine fighting soldier, steadfastly loyal to Napoleon.

MACDONALD, MARSHAL ALEXANDRE (1765–1840)
Leading an Italian corps he broke the Austrian centre at Wagram and was promoted marshal on the battlefield; he joined group demanding Napoleon's abdication in 1814.

MACK, GENERAL KARL LEIBERICH, BARON (1752–1828)
Austrian quartermaster general and senior commander on Danube 1805, where, outmanoeuvred by Napoleon, he surrendered his army at Ulm.

MASSENA, MARSHAL ANDRÉ (1758–1817)
One of the ablest and most rapacious commanders of the Revolution and Empire; he was appointed marshal in 1804 and commanded in Italy in 1805; outstanding in 1809; he was checked in the Peninsula.

Marshal André Massena

MÉLAS, GENERAL MICHAEL FRIEDRICH (1729–1806)
Commanded Austrian forces in northern Italy, defeated at Marengo.

METTERNICH, KLEMENS LOTHAR, PRINCE (1773–1859)
Habsburg diplomat and after 1809 Chancellor; initially favoured
rapprochement with Napoleon, but in summer 1813 led Austria into
Sixth Coalition.

MONCEY, MARSHAL BON-ADRIEN (1754–1842)
Successfully fought Spaniards 1792–5; general of division 1794;
promoted marshal 1804, but after 1809 held primarily administrative
positions.

MOORE, LIEUTENANT GENERAL SIR JOHN (1761–1809)
Reformed light infantry tactics; commanded British expedition in
Peninsula 1808, but compelled to retreat and was killed at Corunna
while covering the embarkation of his troops.

MOREAU, GENERAL JEAN-VICTOR (1763–1813)
Victor at Hohenlinden, rival to Napoleon; involved in royalist
intrigue, exiled 1804; ultimately adviser to Tsar Alexander; died of
wounds sustained at Dresden.

MORTIER, MARSHAL ADOLPHE-ÉDOUARD (1768–1835)
A sound commander, he became marshal 1804; did well
commanding corps 1805, thereafter held various assignments.

**MURAT, MARSHAL JOACHIM,
KING OF NAPLES** (1767–1815)
A charismatic cavalry officer, married
Caroline Bonaparte 1802; made marshal
1804; king of Naples 1808; prominent
in great campaigns, defected 1813
and next year led his army against
Eugène; 1815 his offer to join
Napoleon rejected, conducted his
own campaign in Italy where he was
captured and shot.

Marshal Joachim Murat

NEY, MARSHAL MICHEL (1769–1815)
A brave officer and fine troop leader, marshal 1804, Ney was an ideal corps commander; 1814 led marshals demanding Napoleon's abdication and served Bourbons, but rejoined Napoleon; commanded left wing of Armée du Nord at Quatre Bras but was dilatory and failed as battle commander at Waterloo.

Marshal Michel Ney

ORANGE, WILLIAM, PRINCE (1792–1849)
Commanded corps in Wellington's army at Quatre Bras and Waterloo.

OUDINOT, MARSHAL NICOLAS-CHARLES (1767–1847)
General of division 1799, led Lannes's corps after Aspern–Essling, became marshal after battle of Wagram; joined other marshals to force Napoleon's abdication in 1814.

PAUL I, TSAR OF RUSSIA (1754–1801)
An unstable autocrat, joined Second Coalition, but withdrew following disagreements with Allies; assassinated 1801.

PONIATOWSKI, MARSHAL JOSEF ANTON, PRINCE (1763–1813)
Commander of Polish legion in French service and 1808 War Minister, Grand Duchy of Warsaw; led Polish–Saxon corps 1812–13, marshal 1813; drowned during retreat from Leipzig.

RADETSKY, GENERAL JOSEPH, COUNT (1766–1858)
An able Austrian general, chief of quartermaster general staff after 1809; he served as chief of staff to Schwarzenberg 1813–14.

RAPP, GENERAL JEAN (1771–1821)
A much-wounded aide to Bonaparte, he performed spectacular combat missions; 1815 successfully commanded tiny Army of the Rhine.

REYNIER, GENERAL EBENEZER (1771–1814)
Commanded Saxon Corps in Germany 1813 and after its defection was taken prisoner.

ROBESPIERRE, MAXIMILIEN DE (1758–94)
Uncompromising leader of Jacobin faction; powerful member of Committee of Public Safety after 1793, utilized the Terror against internal and external enemies; was overthrown and executed in July 1794.

SCHARNHORST, GENERAL GERHARD JOHANN DAVID VON (1755–1813)
Appointed Director of the War Department 1808, became major reformer of Prussian Army; intellectual soldier, authored influential writings on military–political topics.

SCHWARZENBERG, FIELD MARSHAL KARL PHILIPP, PRINCE (1771–1820)
Austrian soldier–diplomat, managed to extract Austrian auxiliary corps from Russia 1812; appointed allied commander-in-chief after Austria joined Sixth Coalition 1813.

SÉRURIER, MARSHAL JEAN-MATHIEU-PHILIBERT (1742–1819)
He joined the army in 1755 at the age of 13 and was a regular officer from 1759; he served the Revolution during 1794–7 and again in 1799 in Italy; he supported Bonaparte's takeover and was appointed honorific marshal 1804.

SUCHET, MARSHAL LOUIS-GABRIEL (1770–1826)
The most successful French commander in Spain; promoted marshal 1811, gained victories and substantial popular support; 1815 commanded the minuscule Army of the Alps.

SUVOROV, FIELD MARSHAL ALEKSANDR VASILYEVICH (1729–1800)
Veteran Russian commander, championed bayonet shock action over firepower; reconquered Italy 1799.

VICTOR, MARSHAL CLAUDE-PERRIN (1764–1841)
Received corps command January 1807, marshal in July; served in Spain and Russia, distinguished himself on the Beresina; 1813 fought in Germany.

WELLESLEY, FIELD MARSHAL SIR ARTHUR, DUKE OF WELLINGTON (1769–1852)
After service in Holland and India, promoted to lieutenant general commanding in the Peninsula 1808; developed deliberate operational style, defeated successive French marshals by 1814; 1815 commanded Anglo-Dutch and allied forces in Belgium, defeating Napoleon at Waterloo.

*Field Marshal
Sir Arthur Wellesley*

WITTGENSTEIN, FIELD MARSHAL LUDWIG, PRINCE (1769–1843)
Commanded column at Austerlitz and at Leipzig.

WÜRMSER, GENERAL DAGOBERT SIGMUND, COUNT (1724–97)
Led repeated efforts to relieve Mantua but was defeated.

YORCK, GENERAL JOHANN DAVID (1759–1830)
Commanded Prussian auxiliary corps in Russia; negotiated Tauroggen Convention in 1812 which led to German defection from French alliance.

YORK, FIELD MARSHAL FREDERICK AUGUSTUS, DUKE OF (1763–1827)
Commander-in-chief of the British Army 1789–1809.

ZIETHEN, GENERAL HANS ERNST KARL, COUNT (1770–1848)
Commanded Prussian I Corps at Ligny and Waterloo.

Further reading

The literature on Napoleon and his times is immense, with new works being added constantly. The following list is highly selective and concentrates on books in English because they are most accessible. A fine introduction to the military aspects is Donald D. Horward (ed.), *Napoleonic Military History. A Bibliography* (New York and London, 1986). Also indispensable is Vincent J. Esposito and John R. Elting, *A Military History and Atlas of the Napoleonic Wars* (New York, 1965). Notable reference works include David G. Chandler, *Dictionary of the Napoleonic Wars* (New York, 1979) and Clive Emsley, *The Longman Companion to Napoleonic Europe* (London, 1993). The standard diplomatic history is Paul W. Schroeder, *The Transformation of European Politics 1763–1848* (Oxford, 1994).

There are several good general studies of warfare before the French Revolution. They include Christopher Duffy, *The Military Experience in the Age of Reason* (London, 1987), the relevant chapters in Peter Paret (ed.), *Makers of Modern Strategy from Machiavelli to the Nuclear Age* (Princeton, 1986) and Russell F. Weigley, *The Age of Battles* (Bloomington, 1991). All are useful both for the Revolutionary and Napoleonic period, as is Gunther E. Rothenberg's comprehensive *The Art of Warfare in the Age of Napoleon* (London, 1977). Difficult, but essential to an understanding of the differences between the wars of the old regime and those of the Revolution and Napoleon, is Carl von Clausewitz, *On War*, Peter Paret and Michael Howard (eds. and trs.) (Princeton, 1976).

On the Revolutionary armies there are Ramsay W. Phipps, *The Armies of the First French Republic* (5 vols.; London, 1926–39), Jean-Paul Bertaud, *The Army of the French Revolution* (Princeton, 1988) and John A. Lynn's important *The Bayonets of the Republic: Motivation and Tactics in the Army of Revolutionary France, 1791–94* (Urbana and Chicago, 1984), while T. C. W. Blanning, *The French Revolutionary Wars 1787–1802* (London, 1996) is superb.

Turning to Napoleon, Spencer Wilkinson, *The Rise of General Bonaparte* (Oxford, 1915) and Robert S. Quimby, *The Background of Napoleonic Warfare* (New York, 1957) remain useful. On Napoleon as a military commander, David G. Chandler's magisterial *The Campaigns of Napoleon* (New York, 1966) remains standard, but deals only with the campaigns he commanded in person. See also Owen Connelly, *Blundering to Glory: Napoleon's Military Campaigns* (Wilmington, 1987), a controversial account. Charles J. Esdaile, *The Wars of Napoleon* (London, 1995) provides a detailed analysis of European responses to French imperialism. How armies fought is explored in Rory Muir, *Tactics and the Experience of Battle in the Age of Napoleon* (New Haven, 1998) and Brent Nosworthy, *With Musket, Cannon and Sword: Battle Tactics of Napoleon and his Enemies* (New York, 1996), while B. P. Hughes, *Firepower: Weapons Effectiveness on the Battlefield 1630 to 1850* (New York, 1974) deals with the weaponry of the period. Harold T. Parker, *Three Napoleonic Battles* (Durham, 1944) systematically analyses the overall setting.

John R. Elting, *Swords around the Throne: Napoleon's* Grande Armée (New York and London, 1988) covers more than the title indicates, while Henry Lachouque and Ann S. K. Brown, *The Anatomy of Glory: Napoleon and his Guard* (London, 1997) has splendid illustrations. David G. Chandler (ed.), *Napoleon's Marshals* (New York, 1987) details the careers of the twenty-six notable soldiers. On Napoleon's satellite troops see Frederick C. Schneid, *Soldiers of Napoleon's Kingdom of Italy* (Boulder, 1995) and John H. Gill, *With Eagles to Glory* (London, 1992).

Regarding Napoleon's opponents, there is a plethora of books on the British. On commanders there are Carola Oman, *Sir John Moore* (London, 1953), Elizabeth Longford, *Wellington: The Years of the Sword* (New York, 1969; re-issued 1996), Paddy Griffith (ed.), *Wellington Commander: the Iron Duke's Generalship* (Chichester, 1986) and Lawrence James, *The Iron Duke: a Military Biography of Wellington* (London, 1992). On the army see Richard G. Glover,

Peninsular Preparation: The Reform of the British Army 1795–1809 (Cambridge, 1963) and Michael Glover, *Wellington's Army in the Peninsula, 1808–1814* (Newton Abbot, 1972).

There is less on the continental powers. For Austria and Archduke Charles see Gunther E. Rothenberg, *Napoleon's Great Adversaries: The Archduke Charles and the Austrian Army, 1792–1814* (London, 1982), for Prussia see Peter Paret, *Yorck and the Era of Prussian Reform 1807–1815* (Princeton, 1966), for Russia there is Christopher Duffy, *Russia's Military Way to the West* (London, 1981) and for Spain Charles J. Esdaile, *The Spanish Army in the Peninsular War* (Manchester, 1988). And of course campaign and battle accounts contain additional material.

On the early campaigns we have Guglielmo Ferrero, *The Gamble: Bonaparte in Italy 1796–1797* (London, 1939) and James C. Herold, *Bonaparte in Egypt* (New York, 1962). Notable works for his later campaigns include Frederick N. Maude, *The Ulm Campaign 1805* (London, 1912), Christopher Duffy, *Austerlitz 1805* (London, 1977), Frederick N. Maude, *The Jena Campaign 1806* (London, 1909) and F. Loraine Petre, *Napoleon's Campaign in Poland, 1806–7* (London, 1901). Charles W. C. Oman, *A History of the Peninsular*

THE BATTLE OF MARENGO, 14 JUNE 1800
With his last reserve, the Consular Guard, barely holding, Bonaparte is saved by General Desaix. Bonaparte and his staff are on the left with Desaix, who would be killed during the attack, in the foreground.

War (7 vols.; London, 1902–30) is comprehensive, but David Gates, *The Spanish Ulcer* (London, 1986) is more accessible. Donald D. Horward, *Napoleon and Iberia: The Twin Sieges of Ciudad Rodrigo and Almeida, 1810* (London, 1994) provides a view from the French side. For the Austrian resurgence in 1809 see F. Loraine Petre, *Napoleon and the Archduke Charles* (London, 1908) and for Wagram see Robert M. Epstein, *Napoleon's Last Victory and the Emergence of Modern War* (Lawrence, 1994).

For 1812 there are Alan W. Palmer, *Napoleon in Russia* (New York, 1967) and George Nafziger, *Napoleon's Invasion of Russia* (Novato, 1988), and for the most spectacular battle Christopher Duffy, *Borodino and the War of 1812* (New York, 1973). For Napoleon's attempt to hold Germany in 1813 see F. Loraine Petre, *Napoleon's Last Campaign in Germany, 1813* (London, 1912) and by the same author *Napoleon at Bay, 1814* (London, 1914). On the same topic there is James P. Lawford, *Napoleon: The Last Campaigns, 1813–1815* (New York, 1977), as well as the selected readings in Antony Brett-Jones (ed. and tr.), *Europe against Napoleon: The Leipzig Campaign, 1813. From Eyewitness Accounts* (London, 1970).

The campaign and battle of Waterloo, of special importance in British military history, have nourished a vast literature. For an overall view of the campaign consult Archibald F. Becke, *Napoleon and Waterloo: The Emperor's Campaign with the Armée du Nord* (revised edn; London, 1995). See also Antony Brett-Jones (ed. and tr.), *The Hundred Days. Napoleon's Last Campaign from Eyewitness Accounts* (New York, 1964). The preliminary battle is covered in Andrew Uffindell, *The Eagle's Last Triumph: Napoleon's Victory at Ligny* (London, 1994). For the experience of the British soldier in this battle see the relevant chapter in John Keegan, *The Face of Battle* (New York, 1976; London, 1995). A revisionist view stressing the Dutch–Belgian contribution to victory can be found in David Hamilton-Williams, *Waterloo: New Perspectives. The Great Battle Reappraised* (London, 1993).

Index

Picture credits

Every effort has been made to contact the copyright holders for images reproduced in this book. The publishers would welcome any errors or omissions being brought to their attention.

Art Archive pp. 2, 16, 43, 56, 76, 128–9, 158, 168–9; Fotomas Index pp. 6, 98, 114, 147, 149; AKG pp. 21, 22, 33, 44–5, 48, 51, 59, 63, 103, 108, 111, 122, 142, 151, 155, 171, 172, 188–9, 190, 216, 218, 219, 221, 222, 223, 224, 225, 230; Peter Newark Pictures pp. 70, 134, 192, 227,

The drawing on p. 29 is drawn and supplied by Arcadia Editions Ltd.